Drackert

Willkommen beim letzten Band der *Wordmaster*-Reihe!

Wie in den bisherigen *Wordmaster*-Bänden gibt es wieder zwei Hauptbestandteile:

1. Die New Words

Für fast alle neuen Vokabeln der Schülerbände B5 und B6 gibt es einen Beispielsatz. Die neue Vokabel kannst du (in der richtigen Form) in die Lücke des Beispielsatzes eintragen. Beim Lesen des Satzes lässt sich oft schon erahnen, welche Vokabel gefragt ist. Falls nicht, lies einfach den entsprechenden deutschen Satz auf der rechten Seite – dort steht die gesuchte Vokabel fett gedruckt.

Für die endgültige Lösung kannst du im „Vocabulary"-Teil des Schülerbuchs nachschauen. Da die Reihenfolge der Vokabeln im *Wordmaster* dieselbe wie im Schülerbuch ist, eignet sich der *Wordmaster* auch ideal als Vokabelheft.

2. Die Übungen

Die meisten neuen, aber auch viele „alte" Vokabeln kommen in den vielseitigen Übungen immer wieder zur Anwendung – und die Übungen sind dabei oft ein echter Rätselspaß! So kannst du dir die Vokabeln auch auf lange Sicht besser merken.

Und nun ... viel Spaß beim Üben!

New words ▸ p. 6

She got a __________ when she saw the snake.	Sie bekam einen **Schock**, als sie die Schlange sah.
Harry Potter lives in a __________ world.	Harry Potter lebt in einer **zauberhaften** Welt.
Many Australian animals live in __________.	Viele australische Tiere leben **im Busch**.
There are trees and __________ in our garden.	In unserem Garten gibt es Bäume und **Büsche**.
Hurry up! The train is __________ leave.	Beeil dich! Der Zug ist **im Begriff** abzufahren!
He slept in a __________ in a small tent.	Er schlief in einem **Schlafsack** in einem kleinen Zelt.
Today the __________ are ideal for surfing.	Heute sind die **Wellen** ideal zum Surfen.
I can't __________ this bag. It's too heavy!	Ich kann die Tasche nicht **tragen**. Sie ist zu schwer!
I'll buy steaks and sausages for our __________.	Ich kaufe Steaks und Würstchen für unser **Grillfest**.
Don't drink any __________ when you drive.	Trink keinen **Alkohol**, wenn du fährst.
John is a __________ English name.	John ist ein **weit verbreiteter** englischer Name.
You can all sleep ________ my __________.	Ihr könnt alle **bei** mir **zu Hause** übernachten.
Our school website has a photo __________.	Unsere Schul-Webseite hat eine Bilder**gallerie**.
The Australian __________ is hot and dry.	Das australische **Hinterland** ist heiß und trocken.

1 Scrambled words: Australia

Die Buchstaben auf der linken Seite der Anzeigetafel ergeben Wörter, die etwas mit Australien zu tun haben. Trage die gefundenen Wörter in die mittlere Spalte der Tafel ein. Die Tipps helfen dir.

			TIP
1	ORANGAKO		a typical Australian animal
2	HET HUSB		where these animals live
3	SAWEV		movement of the sea
4	ETH TOKUCAB		the middle of Australia
5	BEERBAUC		party with meat and sausages
6	CARRYPESSK		a very tall building

New words ▸ p. 8

This ____________ should be 7, not 10.5.	Diese **Zahl** sollte 7 und nicht 10,5 sein.
The total __________ of the US is 9,629,091 km².	Die Gesamt**fläche** der USA beträgt 9.629.091 km².
Native Australians were called ______________.	Ureinwohner Australiens nannte man **Aborigines**.
Some ___________ people still hunt in the bush.	Manche **Aborigines** jagen immer noch im Busch.
AIDS is a terrible ____________.	AIDS ist eine schlimme **Krankheit**.
Canada was once a British ____________.	Kanada war einmal eine britische **Kolonie**.
A lot of ____________ were sent to Australia.	Viele **Strafgefangene** schickte man nach Australien.
Australia is a ____________ British colony.	Australien ist eine **ehemalige** britische Kolonie.
Asia is the largest of the five ____________.	Asien ist der größte der fünf **Kontinente**.
Today India is ______________ from Britain.	Indien ist heute **unabhängig** von Großbritannien.
Joe is a __________ friend. I know him very well.	Joe ist ein **enger** Freund. Ich kenne ihn sehr gut.
Does the company ______________ with China?	**Treibt** die Firma **Handel** mit China?

2 Definitions

Vervollständige die Definitionen mit Wörtern aus dem linken Display.
Trage die richtige Lösung aus dem anderen Display in die rechte Spalte ein.

1 a country or *area* under the ______________ of another country *colony*

2 the final ______________ of a speech or an ______________ ______________

3 a person who is guilty of a ___________ and has been sent to ___________ ______________

4 a large area of ______________, like Europe, ______________ or Africa ______________

5 everything that is inside a ______________, a box, etc. ______________

6 a group of pictures, ___________, etc. that someone has in one ___________ ______________

New words ▸ p. 9

He stayed in ________________ the bad weather.	Sie blieb zu Hause **wegen** des schlechten Wetters.
The ________________ protects us from the sun.	Die **Ozonschicht** schützt die Erde vor der Sonne.
________________ are dangerous for your skin.	**Ultraviolette Strahlen** sind gefährlich für die Haut.
You can get __________ from smoking.	Vom Rauchen kann man **Krebs** bekommen.
Put on ______________ when you lie in the sun!	Nimm **Sonnenschutzmittel** zum Sonnenbaden!
The Sahara is a huge __________.	Die Sahara ist eine riesige **Wüste**.
An __________ is a big bird that can't fly.	Ein **Emu** ist ein großer, flugunfähiger Vogel.
We saw lots of fish in the coral __________.	Wir sahen viele Fische im Korallen**riff**.
A __________ is a very intelligent sea animal.	Ein **Delfin** ist ein sehr intelligentes Meerestier.
Moby Dick was a white __________.	Moby Dick war ein weißer **Wal**.
The price of petrol went up __________ five cents.	Der Benzinpreis stieg **um** fünf Cent.

3 More about ... Australia

Vervollständige den Text mit den passenden Wörtern aus der Box.

Aboriginal – beaches – cancer – continent – desert – emu – independent – population – snakes – ultraviolet rays

Australia is also known as 'the fifth (1) ______________' and has an area almost as large as Europe. But with 21.2 million people, Australia's (2) ______________ is only about one quarter of Germany's! It's a former British colony, which became (3) ______________ in 1901. Today, most people live in the big cities on the coast, while only a few Australians live in the bush or the (4) ______________.

A lot of people go to see Ayers Rock, which is a huge, red rock right in the middle of Australia. The rock actually belongs to the (5) ______________ people in that area. Climbing it can be dangerous: sometimes tourists collapse on their way up because it is so hot!

Tourists love Australia because of the beautiful (6) ______________, fantastic landscapes and interesting animals, like the kangaroo, the koala and the (7) ______________. But you should be careful: some animals are very dangerous, like spiders, (8) ______________ or salt-water crocodiles. And don't spend too much time in the sun. The (9) ______________ are very strong in Australia, which means that you can easily get skin (10) ______________!

New words ▸ pp. 10–11

A high ____________ of Germans have a car.	Ein hoher **Prozentsatz** der Deutschen hat ein Auto.
This ____________ compares four countries.	Dieses **Balkendiagramm** vergleicht vier Länder.
The ____________ shows the percentages.	Das **Tortendiagramm** zeigt die Prozentsätze.
Some animals eat grass, ______ horses and cows.	Einige Tiere fressen Gras, **z.B.** Pferde und Kühe.
Let's ________ the cake into two halves.	Lass uns den Kuchen in zwei Hälften **aufteilen.**
Please cut me another ________ of bread.	Schneide mir bitte noch eine **Scheibe** Brot ab.
Wait a minute! I've ________ finished.	Einen Moment! Ich bin **fast** fertig.
In autumn the ________ become yellow and red.	Im Herbst werden die **Blätter** gelb und rot.
She had a rucksack on her ________.	Sie trug einen Rucksack auf dem **Rücken.**
She danced in a ________ at the opera.	Sie tanzte in einem **Ballet** an der Oper.
Tom wants to ____________ and have kids.	Tom will **heiraten** und Kinder kriegen.

4 Words with different meanings

Finde auf der Liste (Seestern-Magnet) ein passendes Wort zu den beiden Sätzen/Satzteilen auf den Zetteln 1–9. Trage es dort ein und unterstreiche die beiden deutschen Entsprechungen.

1)
a) Im australischen <u>Busch</u> gibt es Schlangen.
b) Der <u>Strauch</u> hat gelbe Blätter.
bush

2)
a) Meine Freundin wohnt nahe bei mir.
b) Wir sind sehr enge Freunde.
____

3)
a) in der Gegenwart leben
b) Ich habe ein Geschenk für dich.
____

4)
a) auf einer Welle surfen
b) zum Abschied winken
____

5)
a) Mein Rücken tut weh!
b) Komm zurück!
____

6)
a) Ich erinnere mich daran.
b) Kannst du dir das merken?
____

7)
a) die Fläche eines Landes
b) Sie wohnt in einer schönen Gegend.
____

8)
a) Der Baum hat keine Blätter.
b) Der Zug fährt um 10 Uhr ab.
____

9)
a) Die Preise stiegen um 5 Prozent.
b) Wir fahren mit dem Auto.
____

area
back
~~bush~~
by
close
leaves
present
remember
wave

New words ▸ *pp. 12–13*

Turn around – this road is going ___________ .	Kehr um – diese Straße führt **nirgendwohin.**
Sydney was great, ___________ it was too hot.	Sydney war toll, **obwohl** es zu heiß war.
Now be ___________ – did you take his money?	Sei mal **ehrlich** – hast du sein Geld genommen?
I work on a _________________ in the outback.	Ich arbeite auf einer **Schaffarm** im Hinterland.
The work was hard, but ___________ he liked it.	Die Arbeit war schwer, aber sie gefiel ihm **dennoch.**
A ___________ is good for riding on any ground.	Ein **Geländemotorrad** fährt auf jedem Boden gut.
She cleaned the ___________ off her shoes.	Sie säuberte den **Dreck** von ihren Schuhen.
I'll ___________ a photo to the e-mail.	Ich **hänge** ein Foto **an** die E-Mail.
When you do ___________ , you fall at 190 km/h.	Beim **Fallschirmspringen** fällt man 190 km/h schnell.
___________ is a short form for Australian.	**Aussie** ist eine Kurzform für Australier.

5 Word pairs

Welche Wörter passen zusammen?

1) wear — jeans

2) become — ___

3) thank — ___

4) join — ___

5) put on — ___

6) die of — ___

7) carry — ___

8) set — ___

9) do — ___

10) ride — ___

business
cancer
a club
a dirt bike
God
independent
~~jeans~~
a suitcase
sunscreen
a trap

New words ► pp. 14–15

After the break we'll ________ our lesson.	Nach der Pause **machen** wir **weiter** mit der Stunde.
We had a short ____________ about sport.	Wir hatten ein kurzes **Gespräch** über Sport.
May I __________ myself? My name's Sue.	Darf ich mich **vorstellen**? Ich heiße Sue.
Sorry, could you ________ that, please?	Verzeihung, könnten Sie das bitte **wiederholen**?
I didn't ________ that. Say it again, please.	Ich habe das nicht **verstanden.** Nochmal, bitte!
What can I do? This is a ________ problem.	Was kann ich tun? Das ist ein **heikles** Problem.
The water is cold, so wear a __________!	Das Wasser ist kalt, also trag einen **Surfanzug**!

6 Word building

Verbinde die Wörter 1–10 mit jeweils einem passenden Wort aus der Mauer. Achte dabei auf die Schreibweise (getrennt oder zusammen), und trage die deutsche Übersetzung ein.

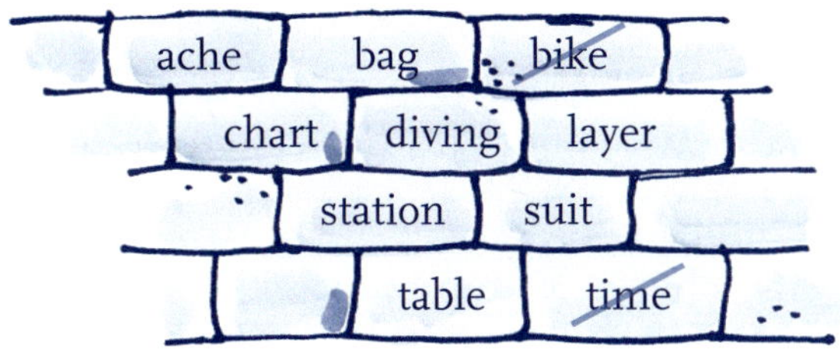

1 dirt bike ________ Geländemotorrad ________

2 lifetime ________ ________

3 sheep ________ ________

4 pie ________ ________

5 sky ________ ________

6 ozone ________ ________

7 stomach ________ ________

8 wet ________ ________

9 time ________ ________

10 sleeping ________ ________

7 Word friends

Auf jedem Plakat gibt es drei Wörter/Wortverbindungen, die direkt nach dem Verb auf dem kleinen Zettel folgen können. Unterstreiche sie.

New words ▸ p. 16

Immigrants __________ in foreign countries.	Einwanderer **siedeln** in fremden Ländern.
We all share the __________ in human rights.	Wir alle teilen den **Glauben** an die Menschenrechte.
Germany was __________ in 1990.	Deutschland wurde 1990 **vereinigt**.
He left in 1992 – __________ I don't know why.	Er ging 1992 fort – **bis heute** weiß ich nicht, warum.
This family tree shows all my __________.	Dieser Stammbaum zeigt alle meine **Vorfahren**.
You __________ drink lots of water when it's hot.	Du **musst** viel trinken, wenn es heiß ist.
I __________ your opinion, but I don't share it.	Ich **respektiere** deine Meinung, teile sie aber nicht.

8 The best word

Finde das Wort A, B, C oder D, das am besten in die Lücke passt.

A compare B unite C attach D upset

1 We all need to __________ in our fight for freedom!

A Aussies B Aborigines C ancestors D anniversaries

2 Some of the Queen's __________ are actually German.

A honest B tricky C magical D close

3 Don't believe him – he isn't a very __________ person.

A to this day B about to do C to the front D that day

4 It's the band's most successful album __________.

A still B nearly C because of D former

5 Look, it's __________ three o'clock! We're going to be late!

A continued B carried C segregated D settled

6 A lot of Europeans __________ in America.

9 The fourth word

Welches Wort fehlt hier?

1	closed – open	separated – united	*6*	translation – translate	introduction – __________
2	sell – sale	believe – __________	*7*	businessman – suit	surfer – __________
3	left – right	front – __________	*8*	lemonade – soft drink	whisky – __________
4	land – elephant	sea – __________	*9*	anything – nothing	anywhere – __________
5	real – reality	dirty – __________	*10*	Germany – country	Asia – __________

New words ▸ p. 17

Does the older ______________ use laptops?	Benutzt die ältere **Generation** Laptops?
He didn't like black people. He was a __________.	Er hatte etwas gegen Schwarze. Er war ein **Rassist**.
different __________ and ethnic groups	unterschiedliche **Rassen** und ethnische Gruppen
Young people often have dreams and __________.	Junge Leute haben oft Träume und **Ideale**.
Her parents died young – she was an __________.	Ihre Eltern starben früh – sie war eine **Waise**.
He had no idea how to __________ a business.	Er wusste nicht, wie man ein Unternehmen **leitet**.
She can't get married because she's a __________.	Sie kann nicht heiraten, weil sie eine **Nonne** ist.
My bed needs a new ______________.	Mein Bett braucht eine neue **Matratze**.
His hair is dark, but mine is __________.	Seine Haare sind dunkel, aber meine sind **hell**.
I'd like to ______________ for being late.	Ich möchte mich für die Verspätung **entschuldigen**.
When they __________ arrived, it was too late.	Als sie **endlich** eintrafen, war es zu spät.
He __________ me _______ buying a broken car!	Er **brachte** mich **dazu**, ein kaputtes Auto zu kaufen!
You can't __________ him – he's too clever.	Du kannst ihn nicht **reinlegen** – er ist zu clever.
We can transport it by train or __________.	Wir können es per Bahn oder **LKW** transportieren.
My garden has a rabbit-__________ fence.	Mein Garten hat einen kaninchen-**sicheren** Zaun.

10 Opposites

Trage das Gegenteil der fettgedruckten Wörter in die Lücken ein.

1 have **fair** / ____________ hair

2 **stop** / ____________ the lesson

3 be **everywhere** / ____________

4 a **public** / ____________ office

5 get **married** / ____________

6 have **old-fashioned** / ____________ ideas

7 the **departure** / ____________ of a train

8 a **slow** / ____________ car

9 so **much** / ____________ water

10 **falling** / ____________ prices

11 open the **front** / ____________ door

12 be **wealthy** / ____________

13 drink **more** / ____________ orange juice

14 a report on **legal** / ____________ immigrants

15 have an **advantage** / a ____________

16 **push** / ____________ a door

17 the answer is **right** / ____________

18 a **clean** / ____________ window

19 **forget** / ____________ something

20 a **strong** / ____________ man

New words ▸ p. 19

You need at least __________ computer skills.	Du brauchst zumindest Computer-**Grund**kenntnisse.
The job is hard work, but the _________ is good.	Der Job ist schwer, aber die **Bezahlung** ist gut.
Do you know who's the __________ of this dog?	Weißt du, wer der **Besitzer** dieses Hundes ist?
After the meal I helped to __________________ .	Nach dem Essen half ich **das Geschirr abwaschen**.
I gave her my __________ and phone number.	Ich gab ihr meine **Adresse** und Telefonnummer.
The __________ says 'Back in 5 minutes'.	Auf dem **Aushang** steht „In 5 Minuten wieder da".
A teacher __________ about € 40,000 a year.	Ein Lehrer **verdient** etwa € 40.000 im Jahr.

11 Spot the mistakes

In jedem Satz sind zwei Fehler. Unterstreiche und korrigiere sie.

1 It's terrible! It gives just too much cars in this city. There are ____________

2 House prices fell at more than five percentage last year. ____________ ____________

3 Can I introduce me? I'm Jo from London. Here's my adress. ____________ ____________

4 Sorry, have you got an other bed? This matrace is too hard. ____________ ____________

5 She had red hairs, as red as some of the leafs in autumn. ____________ ____________

6 Take notices during class, but don't spent too much time on it. ____________ ____________

12 Making new words

Bilde aus den Buchstaben des Wortes so viele neue Wörter wie möglich. Mindestens 20 Wörter solltest du leicht finden. Wenn du über 50 findest, bist du ein „Buchstabenchampion".

anti, noise,

conversation

13 Crossword

Trage die Übersetzungen der deutschen Wörter ins Rätsel ein.

Across

(1) Schmutz, Dreck
(3) (etwas) wiederholen
(5) grundlegend; Grund-, Haupt-
(6) verdienen
(8) anhängen, anheften
(13) Besitzer/in
(14) trotzdem, dennoch
(15) Waise, Waisenkind
(16) Krankheit

Down

(1) Wüste
(2) Rasse
(3) (etwas) leiten
(4) Bezahlung, Lohn
(7) schließlich, endlich
(9) obwohl
(10) fortsetzen, weitermachen
(11) weit verbreitet, häufig
(12) verzwickt, heikel
(14) Scheibe, Stück

14 Pronunciation

Ordne die Wörter der beiden Rapper der richtigen Aussprachegruppe zu, je nachdem, wie der unterstrichene Vokal ausgesprochen wird.

ancestor
honest
alcohol (1)
introduce
because of
Aborigine
(to) continue
~~colony (2)~~
alcohol (2)
dolphin
apologize (2)
colony (1)
convict
common (1)
continent
common (2)
apologize (1)
shock

ə	ɒ
colony (2)	

New words ▸ *p. 32*

________ to become a teacher takes two years.	Die **Ausbildung** zum Lehrer dauert zwei Jahre.
What kind of ________ is a GCSE?	Was für ein **Abschluss** ist ein GCSE?
She's doing an ________ as a hairdresser.	Sie macht eine **Lehre** als Frisörin.
As an ________, you learn at work.	Als **Lehrling** lernt man bei der Arbeit.
Choosing my job was a difficult ________.	Meine Berufswahl war eine schwere **Entscheidung**.
The ________ of the restaurant cooks excellently.	Der **Koch** des Restaurants macht tolles Essen.
She's a ________ at our kindergarten.	Sie ist **Erzieherin** in unserem Kindergarten.
The car ________ didn't find his tools.	Der Auto**mechaniker** fand sein Werkzeug nicht.
I need to take my car to the ________.	Ich muss mein Auto in die **Werkstatt** bringen.

1 The best word

Finde das Wort A, B, C oder D, das am besten in die Lücke passt.

A	B	C	D	Sentence
instruction	notices	apprentices	information	1 Go on the Internet to find more ________ about jobs.
get	do	make	catch	2 Let's stop the discussion – we have to ________ a decision now.
education	apprentice	training	way	3 You have to do special ________ to become a paramedic.
conversation	continue	continent	convict	4 I've just had a nice ________ with someone from the garage.
around	for	after	up	5 A childcare assistant looks ________ children.
coach	chef	owner	boss	6 The mechanic asked his ________ for more pay.
earned	began	received	won	7 In 2010 he ________ an apprenticeship as a chef.
qualification	ancestor	generation	orphan	8 What ________ do I need to do this job?
upset	settle	turn up	run	9 Later, I would like to ________ my own hotel.

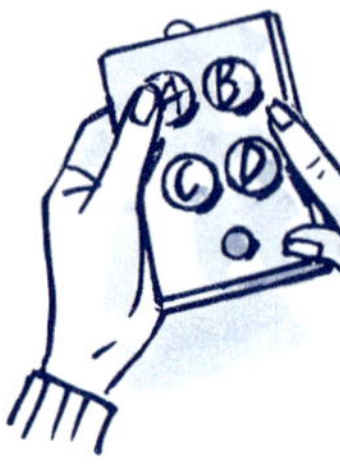

New words ▸ p. 33

A ____________ knows all the products.	Ein **Kundenberater** kennt alle Produkte.
I ________ you to change your job.	Ich **rate** dir, den Job zu wechseln.
I need your ________: this shirt or that one?	Ich brauche deinen **Rat**: dieses Hemd oder jenes?
The ______________ prepared her face.	Der **Maskenbildner** machte ihr Gesicht zurecht.
A ____________ showed me the exercises.	Ein **Fitnesstrainer** zeigte mir die Sportübungen.
He's always tired because he works ________.	Er ist immer müde, weil er **lange arbeitet**.
Please ________ this customer first.	Bitte **bediene** diesen Kunden zuerst.
My car won't go. Can you ________ it?	Mein Auto fährt nicht. Kannst du es **reparieren**?
She's very ________ – she swims and runs a lot.	Sie ist sehr **sportlich** – sie schwimmt und läuft viel.
This painter has lots of ________ talent.	Dieser Maler hat viel **künstlerisches** Talent.
The event was very well __________.	Die Veranstaltung war sehr gut **organisiert**.
I didn't get nervous. I stayed really ________.	Ich wurde nicht nervös. Ich blieb ganz **ruhig**.

2 The fourth word

Welches Wort fehlt hier?

1	'3' – number	'B' – ____________	*5*	relax – relaxed	organize – ____________
2	reality – real	sport – ____________	*6*	believe – belief	decide – ____________
3	weak – strong	nervous – ____________	*7*	students – teach	customers – ____________
4	dirt – dirty	art – ____________	*8*	music – musician	advice – ____________

3 Lost words

Ergänze die Sätze mit der jeweils korrekten Präposition.
Bei einem der Sätze bleibt die Lücke leer.

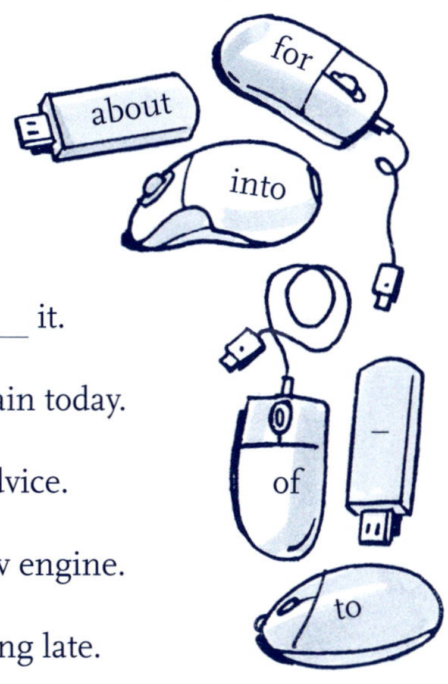

1 I've attached all the photos ____________ my e-mail.

2 She failed the exam, but she was pretty calm ____________ it.

3 Sorry, dear – I have to work ____________ long hours again today.

4 Now let me give you an important piece ____________ advice.

5 The car mechanic tricked me ____________ buying a new engine.

6 When he finally arrived, he apologized ____________ being late.

New words ▸ p. 34

A year abroad develops your ______________ .	Ein Auslandsjahr entwickelt die **Persönlichkeit.**
Take your time. I ______________ waiting.	Lass dir Zeit. **Es macht mir nichts aus**, zu warten.
Believe me! My source is very ______________ .	Glaub mir! Meine Quelle ist sehr **zuverlässig.**
Sad stories __________ me cry.	Traurige Geschichten **bringen** mich **zum** Weinen.
I have a problem which I can't __________ .	Ich habe ein Problem, das ich nicht **lösen** kann.

4 Spot the mistakes

In jedem Satz sind zwei Fehler. Unterstreiche und korrigiere sie.

1 It's no problem – I don't mind to work long times in my job. ______________ ______________

2 He gave me some good advices on how to repare a car. ______________ ______________

3 As make-up artist you have to be calm and good organized. ______________ ______________

4 She's so funny – yesterday she has made me laughing so much! ______________ ______________

5 What do you make in your job? – I am serving people every day. ______________ ______________

5 Word pairs

Welche Wörter passen zusammen?

1) basic ______________

2) earn ______________

3) advise ______________

4) organized ______________

5) run ______________

6) a tricky ______________

7) solve ______________

8) a strong ______________

9) wash ______________

10) work ______________

crime
customers
the dishes
a hotel
long hours
money
personality
a problem
situation
skills

New words ► *p. 35*

Our body is ________ made up of water.	Unser Körper besteht **hauptsächlich** aus Wasser.
I don't feel ______________ on a stage.	Ich fühle mich nicht **selbstsicher** auf einer Bühne.
The new boss is young and __________.	Die neue Chefin ist jung und **tatkräftig**.
My Porsche is as fast as a ______________.	Mein Porsche ist so schnell wie ein **Rennwagen**.
She likes animals – she's a ______________.	Sie liebt Tiere – sie ist **Tierarzthelferin**.
The ______________ helped pull the tooth.	Der **Zahnarzthelfer** half den Zahn zu ziehen.
Maths is easy. It's all very __________.	Mathe ist leicht. Alles ist sehr **logisch**.
Today, cars are full of modern ____________.	Heute sind Autos voll mit moderner **Technologie**.
The __________ finished the house in 1 year.	Die **Bauarbeiter** stellten das Haus in 1 Jahr fertig.
The computer ___________ repaired my PC.	Der Computer**techniker** reparierte meinen PC.
The bus was late, but the train was _________.	Der Bus kam zu spät, aber der Zug war **pünktlich**.
The ___________ took the money I had saved.	Der **Bankangestellte** nahm mein gespartes Geld.
A ________ works in a hospital.	Eine **Krankenschwester** arbeitet im Krankenhaus.

6 Scrambled words: Describing people

Die Buchstaben auf der linken Seite der Anzeigetafel ergeben Wörter, mit denen man Menschen beschreiben kann. Trage die gefundenen Wörter in die mittlere Spalte der Tafel ein. Die Tipps helfen dir.

	✈ (departure)	✈ (arrival)	TIP
1	CENTINDOF		believing in yourself
2	CENTIGERE		full of energy
3	LAMC		not nervous or excited
4	PYROTS		enjoying tennis, climbing, etc.
5	UPLUNACT		never late
6	CARSITTI		good at art
7	AREBELLI		always doing things correctly
8	COGALLI		combining facts when thinking

New words ▸ pp. 36–37

Don't let the dog out. It has to stay ___________.	Lass den Hund nicht raus. Er muss **drinnen** bleiben.
This job ___________ fits perfectly to me.	Dieses Job-**Profil** passt perfekt zu mir.
Write an _______________ if you want the job.	Schreib eine **Bewerbung**, wenn du den Job willst.
You need to fill in an application ___________.	Du musst ein Bewerbungs**formular** ausfüllen.
It's the band's best song ___________.	Es ist das **bis heute** beste Lied der Band.

7 Word search: Jobs

Finde 30 Berufe und übersetze sie ins Deutsche. (↓ →)

V	D	N	G	U	I	D	E	W	B	M	P	A	R	A	M	E	D	I	C	Q	Z	F	A
E	E	K	T	T	A	G	E	U	P	H	O	T	O	G	R	A	P	H	E	R	I	C	R
T	N	A	C	A	R	E	T	A	K	E	R	J	T	T	E	A	C	H	E	R	N	H	T
M	T	S	Z	R	A	C	T	O	R	Y	P	O	L	I	C	E	M	A	N	P	S	E	I
J	I	S	D	E	T	E	C	T	I	V	E	U	H	M	E	D	I	T	O	R	T	M	S
D	S	I	F	Q	W	G	C	H	E	F	Z	R	E	N	G	I	N	E	E	R	R	I	T
O	T	S	I	H	K	J	H	Z	T	F	G	N	F	A	R	M	E	R	C	R	U	S	J
C	K	T	R	S	P	A	I	N	T	E	R	A	W	A	I	T	R	E	S	S	C	T	Y
T	Q	A	E	N	U	R	S	E	X	P	C	L	E	A	N	E	R	S	L	Y	T	H	A
O	H	N	M	S	C	B	T	E	C	H	N	I	C	I	A	N	C	B	O	N	O	M	X
R	S	T	A	A	D	V	I	S	E	R	B	S	U	B	O	D	Y	G	U	A	R	D	P
P	V	L	N	M	E	C	H	A	N	I	C	T	I	P	B	U	I	L	D	E	R	Y	V

actor – Schauspieler/in

New words ▸ *p. 38 (part 1)*

Put these skills on your ___________.	Schreib diese Fertigkeiten in deinen **Lebenslauf**.
How old are you? What's your date of ___________?	Wie alt bist du? Was ist dein **Geburts**datum?
___________ here means 'man' or 'woman'.	**Geschlecht** bedeutet hier „Mann" oder „Frau".
What ___________ are you? – I'm British.	Welche **Nationalität** haben Sie? – Ich bin Brite.
W5 2DU is the ___________ of the London hotel.	W5 2DU ist die **Postleitzahl** des Londoner Hotels.
In ___________ you learn to read and write.	In der **Grundschule** lernt man Lesen und Schreiben.
At the age of 11 you go to ___________.	Mit 11 geht man auf die **weiterführende Schule**.
He gave ___________ till an ambulance arrived.	Er leistete **Erste Hilfe**, bis ein Krankenwagen kam.
At the end of the course he got a ___________.	Am Ende des Kurses bekam er ein **Zertifikat**.
You mustn't drive without a ___________.	Ohne **Führerschein** darf man nicht fahren.
He did a week's ___________ at the bank.	Er machte ein einwöchiges **Praktikum** in der Bank.
She attached a ___________ from her last job.	Sie fügte eine **Referenz** ihres letzten Jobs bei.
I read your job ___________ in *The Times*.	Ich habe Ihre Stellen**anzeige** in der *Times* gelesen.
Should cigarettes be ___________ on TV?	Sollte man im Fernsehen für Zigaretten **werben**?
Most ___________ want to sell something.	Die meisten **Inserenten** wollen etwas verkaufen.

8 Word building

Verbinde die Wörter 1–10 mit jeweils einem passenden Wort aus der Mauer. Achte dabei auf die Schreibweise (getrennt oder zusammen), und trage die deutsche Übersetzung ein.

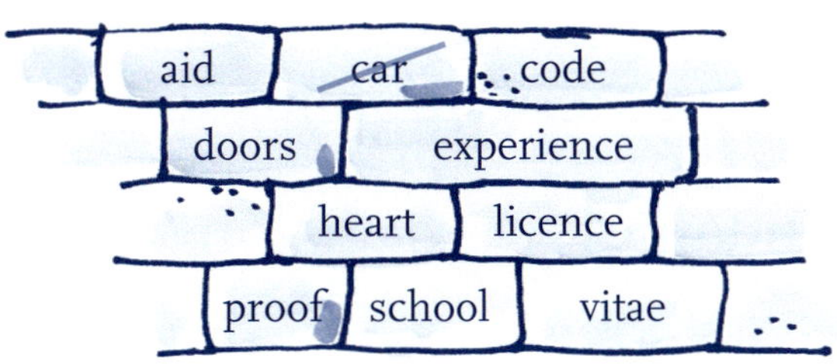

1 racing car ___________ ___________	*6* curriculum ___________ ___________
2 primary ___________ ___________	*7* water ___________ ___________
3 work ___________ ___________	*8* sweet ___________ ___________
4 post ___________ ___________	*9* in ___________ ___________
5 first ___________ ___________	*10* driving ___________ ___________

New words ▸ pp. 38 (part 2)–39

Don't forget to ___________ your CV.	Vergiss nicht, deinen Lebenslauf **beizulegen.**
I'll be ___________ to send you my references.	**Gerne** schicke ich Ihnen meine Referenzen.
Her CD is now ___________ at all music shops.	Ihre CD ist jetzt in allen Musikläden **verfügbar.**
A real friend is there for you ___________ .	Ein echter Freund ist **jederzeit** für dich da.
Never write 'I'm' or 'he's' in ___________ letters.	Schreibe nie „I'm" oder „he's" in **förmlichen** Briefen.
E-mails are often more ___________ than letters.	Emails sind oft **informeller** als Briefe.
Use a formal ___________ in an application.	Verwende förmlichen **Stil** in einer Bewerbung.
Beginning of a letter: ___________ ,	Briefbeginn: **Sehr geehrte Damen und Herren,**
Is this Harry Potter film ___________ to the book?	Ist dieser Harry Potter Film **ähnlich** wie das Buch?
A ___________ film is about plants and animals.	Ein **Natur**film handelt von Pflanzen und Tieren.
A company is run by the ___________ .	Eine Firma wird vom **Geschäftsführer** geleitet.
In ___________ jobs you need to think logically.	In **technischen** Berufen muss man logisch denken.
The farmer drove the ___________ across the field.	Der Bauer fuhr den **Traktor** über das Feld.
The car is a masterpiece of ___________ .	Das Auto ist ein Meisterwerk des **Ingenieurswesens.**
My ___________ of English? I'm a beginner.	Mein Englisch**niveau**? Ich bin Anfänger.
The ___________ of drugs in sport is a problem.	Der **Gebrauch** von Drogen im Sport ist ein Problem.

9 Word stress

Unterstreiche bei allen Wörtern die Silbe, die betont werden muss.

address	advertise	advertisement	application
available	certificate	confident	decision
enclose	energetic	engineering	formal
garage	indoors	nationality	nature
organized	profile	qualification	reference
reliable	similar	technical	technology

New words ▸ *p. 40*

The ______________ went well – he got the job!	Das **Vorstellungsgespräch** lief gut – er hat den Job!
They gave the job to the other ________________ .	Sie gaben dem anderen **Kandidaten** den Job.
His sports car didn't ___________ her much.	Sein Sportwagen **beeindruckte** sie nicht besonders.
___________ well for the opera – no jeans, please!	**Zieh** dich gut für die Oper an – bitte keine Jeans!
He's a ______________ candidate for the job.	Er ist ein **geeigneter** Kandidat für den Job.
Her main ______________ ? She's very reliable.	Ihre Haupt**stärke**? Sie ist sehr zuverlässig.
Tell us a strength and a _______________ of yours.	Sag uns eine Stärke und eine **Schwäche** von dir.
We do an ___________________ of the candidates.	Wir führen eine **Beurteilung** der Kandidaten durch.
It's difficult to ___________ the new situation.	Es ist schwer, die neue Lage **einzuschätzen**.
Please write on an empty ___________ of paper.	Bitte schreib auf ein leeres **Blatt** Papier.
She had a sad ___________ in her eyes.	Sie hatte einen traurigen **Ausdruck** in ihren Augen.
He's eaten your chocolate? That's ___________ !	Er hat deine Schokolade gegessen? Das ist **frech**!

10 More about ... Networks on the Internet

Vervollständige den Text mit den passenden Wörtern aus der Box.

application – candidates – cheeky – dangerous – impress –
interview – join – look – opinions – profiles – reliable – suitable

Every day, lots of young people (1) ________________ a network on the Internet. They put their names and (2) ________________ online, give their (3) ________________ on personal questions, or put on pictures that are not (4) ________________ for everyone.

These networks can be highly (5) ________________ . Companies which are looking for new people often check the Internet to find out more about the (6) ________________ . So if you have sent off an (7) ________________ and hope to be invited to a job (8) ________________ , make sure you know exactly what you have put on the Internet. Remember that it will not (9) ________________ your future boss to see those (10) ________________ pictures of you completely drunk at a party, or the one with that stupid (11) ________________ on your face. They will simply think that you are not a very (12) ________________ person!

New words ▸ pp. 42–44

The captain gave the ________________ to stop.	Der Kapitän gab den **Befehl**, zu stoppen.
He sent the service team a __________ for help.	Er schickte eine **Bitte** um Hilfe an das Serviceteam.
As a _______________, you sell holidays.	Als **Reisebürokauffrau** verkauft man Urlaubsreisen.
I didn't __________ in the last election.	Ich bin nicht **zur** letzten **Wahl gegangen**.
The __________ of the new car looks great.	Das **Design** des neuen Autos sieht toll aus.
They changed the __________ of the article.	Sie änderten den **Aufbau** des Artikels.
Can I __________ your pen, please?	Kann ich bitte deinen Stift **ausleihen**?
Don't worry! I can __________ you the money.	Keine Sorge! Ich kann dir das Geld **leihen**.
The show was sold out __________ one week!	Die Show war **innerhalb** einer Woche ausverkauft!
'Everything ______________ better,' says Grandpa.	„**Früher war** alles besser“, sagt Opa.
You will __________ your money within two days.	Sie **erhalten** Ihr Geld innerhalb von zwei Tagen.
He paid by filling in a __________ for € 100.	Er zahlte mit einem **Scheck** über € 100.

11 Opposites

Trage das Gegenteil der fettgedruckten Wörter in die Lücken ein.

1 stay **outdoors** / ____________

2 be very **shy** / ____________

3 **divide** / ____________ a country

4 always be **late** / ____________

5 the **wrong** / ____________ way

6 **lend** / ____________ some money

7 the **death** / ____________ of someone

8 my main **strength** / ____________

9 write **formal** / ____________ letters

10 **send** / ____________ an e-mail

12 Odd word out

Ein Wort passt nicht.
Finde und unterstreiche es.

1 tiger – dolphin – bear – lion

2 vote – take – grab – borrow

3 style – design – layout – cheque

4 tractor – racing car – garage – truck

5 manager – leader – chef – boss

6 birth – question – candidate – interview

7 tricky – cheeky – hard – difficult

8 training – apprenticeship – sex – work experience

9 CV – postcode – reference – certificate

10 reliable – punctual – organized – close

New words ▸ *pp. 45–46*

Are you ____________ about the future?	Bist du **zuversichtlich** für die Zukunft?
He won't trick you – you can ____________ him.	Er legt dich nicht rein – du kannst ihm **trauen**.
How did she ____________ to the news?	Wie hat sie auf die Nachricht **reagiert**?
Everybody was ____________ by the terrorist attack.	Alle waren von dem Terrorangriff **schockiert**.
He waited ____________, but then he left.	Er wartete **eine Weile**, aber dann ging er.
We have a clear ____________ at our school.	An unserer Schule gibt es ein klares **Regelwerk**.
The chef likes his new ____________ of knives.	Dem Koch gefällt sein neues Messer**set**.
He wants to be the best – he's so ____________!	Er will der Beste sein – er ist so **ehrgeizig**!
We are ____________ to solve the problem.	Wir sind **entschlossen**, das Problem zu lösen.
Life is ____________ with kids and a job.	Das Leben ist **stressig** mit Kindern und Beruf.
US students ____________ from high school at 16.	US-Schüler **machen** mit 16 den **Schulabschluss**.
Sorry, but I can't give you a ____________ answer.	Ich kann dir leider keine **eindeutige** Antwort geben.
Joe is nice and very ____________ with the girls.	Joe ist sehr nett und sehr **beliebt** bei den Mädchen.
Tim has ended his ____________ with Jennifer.	Tim hat seine **Beziehung** mit Jennifer beendet.
You want even more? Don't be so ____________!	Du willst noch mehr? Sei nicht so **habgierig**!
I'll ____________ what we've said so far.	Ich **fasse zusammen**, was wir bisher gesagt haben.

13 Words with different meanings

Finde die passende englische Übersetzung zu den unterstrichenen deutschen Wörtern auf den Zetteln 1–6.

1)
a) Schau dir diese Zahlenreihe an.
b) Ich möchte einen neuen Satz Teller kaufen.

____

2)
a) Ich bin gern bereit, dir das Geld zu leihen.
b) Ich bin ja so glücklich, dich zu sehen!

____

3)
a) Man hat die Gestaltung des Produkts geändert.
b) Wie findest du den Entwurf für mein Kleid?

____

4)
a) Er war zuversichtlich, die Prüfung zu bestehen.
b) Eigentlich ist sie nicht selbstbewusst, sondern schüchtern.

____

5)
a) Hast du schon feste Pläne fürs Wochenende?
b) Ich kann dir keine endgültige Antwort geben.

____

6)
a) Dieses Buch ist zur Zeit nicht vorrätig.
b) Wann genau sind Sie erreichbar?

____

14 Crossword

Trage die Übersetzungen der deutschen Wörter ins Rätsel ein.

Across
(1) innerhalb von
(3) ruhig
(5) Schulabschluss machen
(7) Klasse
(8) reagieren
(11) entschlossen
(12) Gebrauch
(13) Blatt (Papier)
(15) schockiert
(16) beliebt

Down
(2) Natur
(3) Befehl
(4) jm. etwas leihen
(6) Beziehung
(9) anstrengend
(10) gierig
(13) lösen
(14) vertrauen

15 Two-part verbs

Vervollständige die Sätze mit einem passenden Wort von den USB-Sticks.

1 If you don't know the word, just look it ______________.

2 It's warm in here. Can I take ______________ my coat?

3 I always get ______________ at seven o'clock in the morning.

4 Please turn ______________ the light now – you need to sleep.

5 Sue doesn't want her parents to find ______________ that she has a boyfriend.

6 You have to get ______________ this train at the next station.

7 It's grandpa's birthday. Don't forget to put ______________ your best shirt.

8 Would you like to go ______________ with me on Saturday night?

9 Could you please sum ______________ your main ideas again?

10 He stopped talking for a moment, but then he went ______________.

16 Word groups

Ordne den vier Oberbegriffen auf den Laptops die jeweils sechs am besten passenden Wörter zu. Weitere sechs Wörter aus der Box passen zu keinem der Oberbegriffe.

advert – ambitious – assess – bank clerk – bank robber – ~~candidate~~ – certificate – cheeky – convict – customer adviser – CV – dark – enclose – energetic – form – greedy – helpful – impress – mechanic – nurse – prepare – questions – reef – reference – reliable – suit – tortoise – travel agent – unconscious – vet

candidate

New words ▸ p. 48

A global company sells products ________ .	Ein globale Firma verkauft Produkte **weltweit.**
Sport and no alcohol: that's a healthy ________ .	Sport und kein Alkohol ist ein gesunder **Lebensstil.**
Spain is full of tourists, ________ in summer.	Spanien ist voller Touristen, **besonders** im Sommer.
Can a cat ________ with a dog?	Kann **sich** eine Katze mit einem Hund **anfreunden**?
She loved Tim, but he didn't ________ her.	Sie liebte Tim, aber er **stand** nicht **auf** sie.
I ________ to a policeman and asked for help.	Ich **ging auf** einen Polizisten **zu** und bat um Hilfe.

1 Definitions

Vervollständige die Definitionen mit Wörtern aus dem linken Display.
Trage die korrekte Lösung aus dem anderen Display in die rechte Spalte ein.

1 a small, printed form you use for paying, just like ________ ________
2 a person in your ________ who lived a long ________ ago ________
3 the ________ in which a person or a group of ________ lives ________
4 a ________ who is applying for a ________ ________
5 a ________ where ________ are repaired ________
6 a ________ which gives ________ about your way of working ________
7 a ________ of ________ for writing or printing on ________
8 a serious ________ which grows in your ________ ________

New words ▸pp. 49–50

My daily __________ are quite boring.	Meine täglichen **Pflichten** sind ziemlich langweilig.
In __________, students learn all about electricity.	In **Physik** lernen die Schüler alles über Elektrizität.
Our __________ teacher made a small explosion.	Unser **Chemie**lehrer erzeugte eine kleine Explosion.
There were 16 __________ on my birthday cake.	Auf meiner Geburtstagstorte waren 16 **Kerzen**.
Do students smoke __________ in the toilets?	Rauchen Schüler **heimlich** auf den Toiletten?
Grandpa's __________ was five days after he died.	Opas **Beerdigung** war fünf Tage nachdem er starb.
He never visits her because he feels __________.	Er besucht sie nie, weil er sich **unerwünscht** fühlt.
Time __________ quickly during an exam.	Während einer Prüfung **vergeht** die Zeit schnell.

2 Crossword

Trage die Übersetzungen der deutschen Wörter ins Rätsel ein.

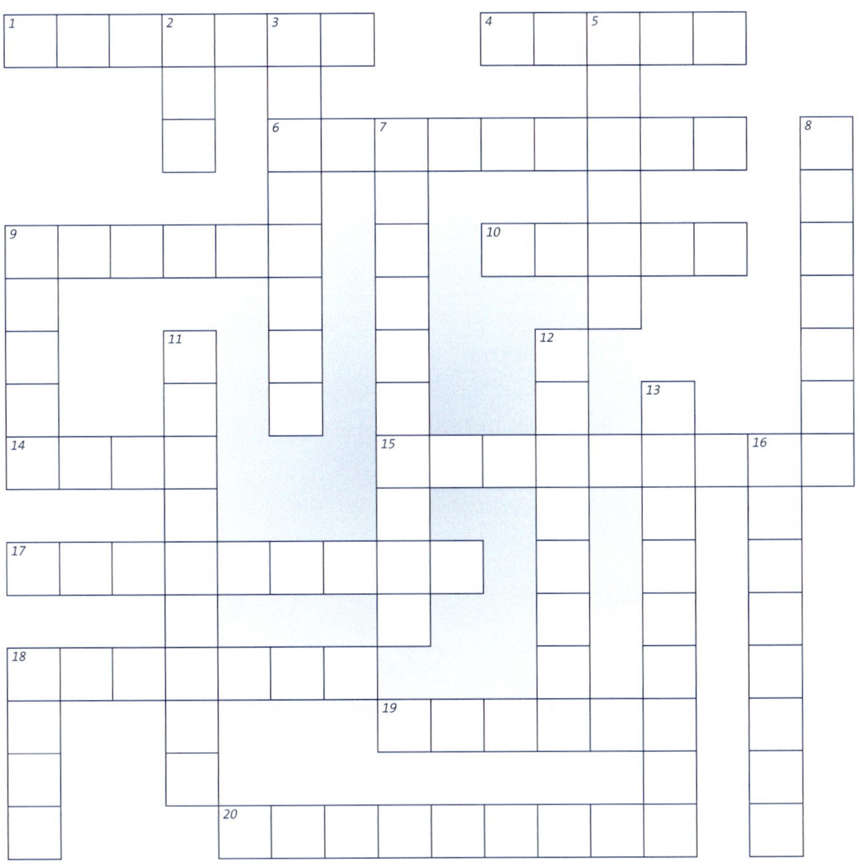

Across
(1) Bitte
(4) auf (jn.) stehen
(6) Chemie
(9) Kerze
(10) Geburt
(14) verdienen (Geld)
(15) ehrgeizig
(17) verfügbar, erreichbar
(18) Beerdigung
(19) frech, dreist
(20) weltweit

Down
(2) Gebrauch, Verwendung
(3) heimlich
(5) Natur
(7) besonders, vor allem
(8) Physik
(9) (Haus-)Arbeit, Pflicht
(11) selbstbewusst / zuversichtlich
(12) passend, geeignet
(13) Lebensstil
(16) unerwünscht, ungewollt
(18) Formular

New words ▸ pp. 51 – 52

First, he gave an __________ of his presentation.	Zuerst stellte er die **Gliederung** seines Vortrags vor.
Today the teacher ______________ a new topic.	Heute hat der Lehrer ein neues Thema **eingeführt**.
Titanic is a good film. ________, it's a bit long.	Der Film *Titanic* ist gut. Er ist **jedoch** etwas lang.
The film was _______ 'not suitable' for children.	Der Film wurde als „für Kinder ungeeignet" **bewertet**.
It's not true – the information was __________ .	Es stimmt nicht – die Information war **falsch**.
He _________ the file under 'mail.doc'.	Er **speicherte** die Datei unter „mail.doc".
You're late again ... ____________, let's go.	Du bist wieder zu spät ... **Aber egal**, lass uns gehen.

3 Words with a similar meaning

Finde Wörter, die das Gleiche bedeuten wie die fettgedruckten Wörter.
Trage sie ein und schreibe die deutsche Übersetzung auf.

1 My father has always been a **supporter** / fan of ManU. Anhänger/in
2 The food was good. **But** / _______________, it was a bit expensive. _______________
3 She's really **afraid** / _______________ of spiders. _______________
4 I liked the **structure** / _______________ of his presentation. _______________
5 The information we had was **wrong** / _______________. _______________
6 He's very **smart** / _______________ for his age. _______________
7 There's a CD shop **not far from** / _______________ the cinema. _______________
8 On this website you can **assess** / _______________ your teachers. _______________

4 Lost words

Ergänze die Sätze mit einem passenden Wort von der Auswahl rechts.
Bei einem der Sätze bleibt die Lücke leer.

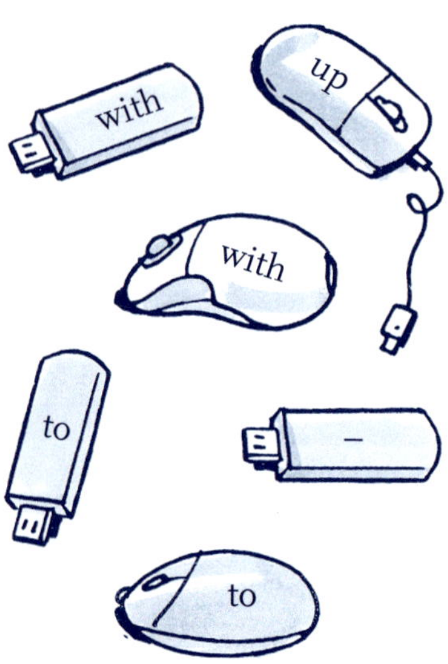

1 The design of the new car is similar __________ the old one.
2 On holiday she made friends __________ a girl from Ireland.
3 Sandra just looks awesome – I really fancy __________ her.
4 I went __________ to her and asked her out on a date.
5 So, how did she react __________ your suggestion?
6 She's very popular __________ all the boys in our class.

New words ► p. 53

The __________ is € 1.20 to the pound.	Der **Wechselkurs** ist € 1,20 für ein Pfund.
I'll just go and get some __________ from the bank.	Ich gehe nur etwas **Bargeld** von der Bank holen.
You can pay cash or by __________.	Du kannst bar oder mit **Kreditkarte** bezahlen.
Here's your change and your __________.	Hier ist das Wechselgeld und Ihre **Quittung**.
Excuse me, I __________ pasta, not rice.	Verzeihung, ich habe Nudeln **bestellt**, nicht Reis.
She took a £20 __________ out of her purse.	Sie nahm einen £ 20-**Schein** aus ihrer Geldbörse.

5 Words with different meanings

Finde die passende englische Übersetzung zu den unterstrichenen deutschen Wörtern auf den Zetteln 1–6.

1)
a) Ich muss die Nummer noch abspeichern.
b) Ich bin sicher, sie werden uns retten.
____

2)

a) Der Tennisplatz ist geschlossen.
b) Er arbeitet am Gericht.
____

3)
a) Wir möchten jetzt bestellen.
b) Das ist die falsche Reihenfolge.

____

4)

a) Ich habe nur einen 100-Euro-Schein.
b) Hast du nicht die Notiz gelesen?
____

5)

a) Heute werden wir ein neues Thema einführen.
b) Darf ich dir Christoph vorstellen?
____

6)
a) Das bedeutet gar nichts.

b) Was meinst du damit?
____

6 Odd word out

Ein Wort passt nicht.
Finde und unterstreiche es.

1 fair – basic – dark – brown

2 receipt – job – chore – work

3 love – like – fancy – order

4 bush – desert – disease – outback

5 candle – cash – credit card – note

6 determined – unwanted – confident – ambitious

7 wrong – false – incorrect – secretly

8 finally – especially – at last – in the end

9 history – chemistry – biology – physics

10 conversation – talk – discussion – lifestyle

New words ▸ p. 54

___________ workers help homeless people.	**Sozial**arbeiter helfen obdachlosen Menschen.
Bullying is anti-social _______________.	Andere zu tyrannisieren ist unsoziales **Verhalten**.
She _____________ as if nothing had happened.	Sie **verhielt sich** so, als ob nichts passiert wäre.
You have to do it! It's an _________ from the boss.	Du musst es tun! Es ist eine **Anordnung** vom Chef.
Should we __________ racist websites?	Sollten wir rassistische Webseiten **sperren**?
She sent him to his room as a _______________.	Als **Strafe** schickte sie ihn auf sein Zimmer.
Do you ___________ your kids for bad behaviour?	**Bestrafst** du deine Kinder für schlechtes Verhalten?
At the age of 18 he _____________ as a chef.	Mit 18 **machte** er **eine Ausbildung** zum Koch.
_____________________ your room! It's so untidy!	**Räum** dein Zimmer **auf**! Es ist so unordentlich!
Is there a ______________ song you want to hear?	Möchtest du ein **bestimmtes** Lied hören?
The murderer had to go to ___________.	Der Mörder musste ins **Gefängnis** gehen.
_____________ is often sprayed on trains.	**Graffiti** wird oft auf Züge gesprüht.
He can't drink because he's ______________.	Er darf nicht trinken, weil er **minderjährig** ist.
Look! Someone has _______________ the car!	Schau! Jemand hat das Auto **mutwillig beschädigt**!
Is graffiti art or __________________?	Ist Graffiti Kunst oder **Vandalismus**?

7 Word families

a) Finde die passenden Nomen zu den angegebenen Verben.

1 assess – ___________________	*4* introduce – ________________	*7* advise – ___________________
2 behave – __________________	*5* vandalize – ________________	*8* save – _____________________
3 punish – __________________	*6* succeed – _________________	*9* imagine – __________________

b) Vervollständige die Sätze mit der korrekten Form eines Verbs oder Nomens aus a).

1 You have no idea? Well, use your _____________________!

2 The band's new album is a huge _____________________.

3 Oh dear! I forgot to _____________________ the file before the program crashed.

4 He didn't _____________________ in finding a new job.

5 If you don't _____________________ yourself, you'll have to go to your room.

New words ▸ p. 55

Smoking can ________ cancer.	Rauchen kann Krebs **verursachen.**
Let's go by bike ____________ taking the car.	Lasst uns mit dem Fahrrad **statt** dem Auto fahren.
I don't like rice. I'll have pasta ________.	Reis mag ich nicht. Ich nehme **stattdessen** Nudeln.
At the age of 14 he __________ his first crime.	Mit 14 Jahren **beging** er sein erstes Verbrechen.
At ______________ he learned to follow rules.	Im **Erziehungslager** lernte er, Regeln zu befolgen.
Wear your _______ – there's water everywhere.	Zieh deine **Stiefel** an – überall ist Wasser.
An _______ is a big bird that can see very well.	Ein **Adler** ist ein großer Vogel, der gut sehen kann.
Do young men have to do __________ service?	Müssen junge Männer zum **Militär**dienst?
The drill __________ shouted at the boy.	Der Militär-**Ausbilder** schrie den Jungen an.
There's always strict _________ in the military.	Beim Militär herrscht immer strenge **Disziplin**.
I'm revising – I want to ________ in the test.	Ich lerne gerade – ich will im Test **gut abschneiden.**

8 Word search: Boot camps and troublemakers

Finde 15 Begriffe aus dem Wortfeld „Erziehungslager/Unruhestifter". (↓ →) Übersetze sie ins Deutsche.

G	V	P	R	I	S	O	N	W	S	F	P
M	V	B	W	G	R	A	F	F	I	T	I
B	A	R	M	I	L	I	T	A	R	Y	N
E	N	U	R	U	L	E	S	K	U	K	S
H	D	I	S	C	I	P	L	I	N	E	T
A	A	T	R	O	U	B	L	E	F	R	R
V	L	I	A	W	I	H	U	G	B	G	U
I	I	Q	R	C	R	I	M	E	I	H	C
O	S	I	D	W	O	R	D	E	R	O	T
U	M	I	V	I	O	L	E	N	C	E	O
R	K	E	B	U	L	L	Y	I	N	G	R
S	A	P	U	N	I	S	H	R	B	A	N

prison – Gefängnis ____________

____________ ____________

____________ ____________

____________ ____________

____________ ____________

____________ ____________

____________ ____________

____________ ____________

New words ▸ pp. 56–57

It's really difficult to __________ what I feel.	Es ist sehr schwer, meine Gefühle **auszudrücken**.
If you don't understand, ask for ______________.	Wenn du es nicht verstehst, bitte um **Klarstellung**.
It __________ me that there's so much violence.	Mich **beunruhigt**, dass es so viel Gewalt gibt.
There's a crowd of __________ outside the disco.	Eine Menge **Jugendlicher** steht vor der Disco.
We must _______ something __________ violence.	Wir müssen etwas gegen die Gewalt **unternehmen**.

9 Verb forms

Ergänze die Tabelle der unregelmäßigen Verben.

1	get	got	got	8	break		
2		rose		9		gave	
3		spoke		10			sat
4	write			11			shone
5			done	12	make		
6	read			13		grew	
7		ran		14			lent

10 Word friends

Auf jedem Plakat gibt es drei Wörter/Wortverbindungen, die direkt nach dem Verb auf dem kleinen Zettel folgen können. Unterstreiche sie.

New words ▸ p. 58

The water is from a clean mountain ___________.	Das Wasser ist aus einer sauberen Berg**quelle**.
I was there ________________ two other people.	Ich war dort **zusammen mit** noch zwei Leuten.
Please put your ____________ in the bin!	Tu deinen **Müll** bitte in die Tonne!
I like Jenny. She's _________ a nice girl!	Ich mag Jenny. Sie ist **so** ein nettes Mädchen!
It's ____________ that I couldn't meet her.	Es ist **ein Jammer**, dass ich sie nicht treffen konnte.
A _________ swims with four legs.	Eine **Wasserschildkröte** schwimmt mit vier Beinen.
I will help you if ever you are in _________.	Ich werde dir helfen, wenn du jemals in **Not** bist.
I think more people should _________ blood.	Ich finde, mehr Menschen sollten Blut **spenden**.
The story of Jesus Christ is in the _________.	Die Geschichte von Jesus Christus ist in der **Bibel**.
This ticket machine only takes _________.	Dieser Fahrkartenautomat nimmt nur **Münzen**.
She put the $10 _________ into her purse.	Sie steckte den $ 10-**Schein** in ihre Geldbörse.
The flight and hotel cost €500 ______________.	Der Flug und das Hotel kosteten **insgesamt** € 500.
_________ fruit is OK, but fresh fruit is better.	Obst **in Dosen** ist OK, aber frisches Obst ist besser.
You can buy cola in _________ or bottles.	Man kann Cola in **Dosen** oder Flaschen kaufen.
You should _________ potatoes cool and dark.	Man sollte Kartoffeln kühl und dunkel **lagern**.
He stayed ___________ in London after the show.	Er blieb **über Nacht** in London nach der Show.

11 Pronunciation

Ordne die Wörter der richtigen Aussprachegruppe zu, je nachdem, wie der unterstrichene Vokal ausgesprochen wird.

~~enclose~~ command chore borrow commit form instructor confident introduce mostly logical note popular prison social solve order organized postcode sporty

əʊ	ɒ	ɔː	ə
enclose			

New words ▸ pp. 59–64

______________ helps old and sick people.	**Gemeinnützige Arbeit** hilft den Alten und Kranken.
We offer our products and __________ online.	Wir bieten unsere Produkte und **Dienste** online an.
We should keep costs down to a __________.	Wir sollten die Kosten auf einem **Minimum** halten.
My dad ______________ me to become a chef.	Mein Vater **ermutigte** mich, Koch zu werden.
Then we had the __________ to ask questions.	Dann hatten wir die **Möglichkeit**, Fragen zu stellen.
July 4th is ______________ Day in America.	Der 4. Juli ist der **Unabhängigkeit**stag in Amerika.
Last year I didn't ______________ my birthday.	Letztes Jahr habe ich nicht Geburtstag **gefeiert**.
Never leave cash or __________ lying around.	Lass nie Geld oder **Wertsachen** herumliegen.
We have to __________ jobs for young people.	Wir müssen Jobs für junge Leute **schaffen**.
The film is a great thriller, full of __________.	Der Film ist ein toller Thriller, voller **Spannung**.

12 The best word

Finde das Wort A, B, C oder D, das am besten in die Lücke passt.

A	B	C	D	
right	trash	wrong	false	1 A turtle lives in the water. True or ______________?
possibility	service	opportunity	possible	2 In London you'll have the ______________ to learn English.
may	can	must	will	3 Can I have a cola, please? – Sure, here's a ______________ for you.
encourage	create	celebrate	donate	4 We should ______________ more students to go abroad for a year.
spring	summer	autumn	winter	5 Don't drink the water from that ______________!
really	particular	finally	especially	6 I like both dresses, ______________ the blue one.

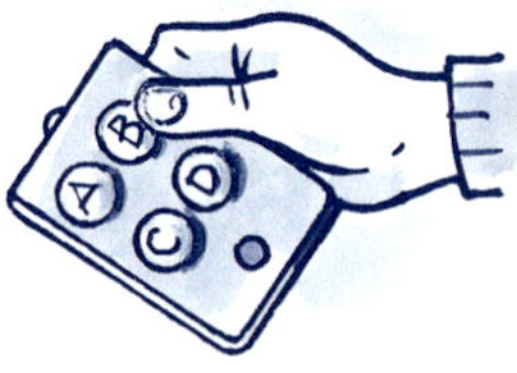

13 Making new words

Bilde aus den Buchstaben des Wortes so viele neue Wörter wie möglich. Wenn du fünf Wörter findest: nicht schlecht. Zehn Wörter: sehr gut. 15 oder mehr Wörter: absolute Spitze!

unwanted

went, and,

14 Spot the mistakes

In jedem Satz sind zwei Fehler. Unterstreiche und korrigiere sie.

1 No problem – you can leave your valuable in our save. ________ ________

2 I'm not wanting a credit card – I always pay by cash. ________ ________

3 The party was a great possibility to meat my old friends. ________ ________

4 Jo can't be in the prison – he's such a well-behaving boy! ________ ________

5 I did pretty good in the test – I got 50 points all together. ________ ________

15 Word building

Verbinde die Wörter 1–8 mit jeweils einem passenden Wort aus der Mauer. Achte dabei auf die Schreibweise (getrennt oder zusammen), und trage die deutsche Übersetzung ein.

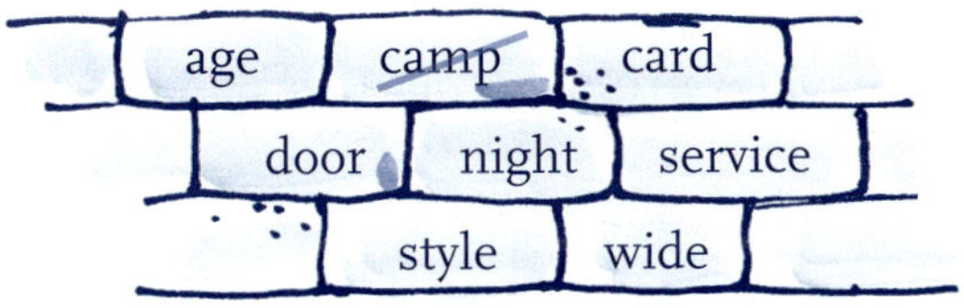

1 boot camp ________

2 life ________ ________

3 over ________ ________

4 under ________ ________

5 community ________ ________

6 world ________ ________

7 back ________ ________

8 credit ________ ________

16 What are the words?

Wie übersetzt man die fettgedruckten Wörter ins Deutsche?

1 She's now in **form** 9PD. ________

2 Please fill in this **form**. ________

3 A summary is a shorter **form** of a text. ________

4 We'd like to **order** now. ________

5 Just put the numbers in the right **order**. ________

6 Sorry, but it's an **order** from the boss. ________

B5 Unit 4

New words ▸ pp. 74 – 76

The lake is so __________ that there are no fish.	Der See ist so **verseucht**, dass es keine Fische gibt.
Does she use oil to make her hair __________ ?	Nimmt sie Öl, um ihr Haar **glänzend** zu machen?
The bus was __________ – we couldn't get on!	Der Bus war **überfüllt** – wir konnten nicht einsteigen!
She found out that her husband had a ________ .	Sie fand heraus, dass ihr Mann eine **Geliebte** hatte.
I met her __________ – three days ago, I think.	Ich traf sie **neulich** – vor drei Tagen, glaube ich.
There weren't many ______________ on board.	Es waren nicht viele **Passagiere** an Bord.
The short train only had three ____________ .	Der kurze Zug hatte nur drei **Waggons**.
He wanted to leave, but she __________ to him.	Er wollte gehen, aber sie **hielt sich** an ihm **fest**.
The baby ________________ for the baby bottle.	Das Baby **griff** nach der Babyflasche.
My room's small – there isn't enough ________ .	Mein Zimmer ist klein – es gibt nicht genug **Platz**.
It was raining, so the ground was __________ .	Es regnete, daher war der Boden **nass**.
Don't touch it – the paint isn't __________ yet.	Fass es nicht an – die Farbe ist noch nicht **trocken**.
__________ believe we will be born again.	**Hindus** glauben, dass wir wiedergeboren werden.
A lot of ____________ celebrate Ramadan.	Viele **Muslime** feiern Ramadan.
______________ believe in Jesus Christ.	**Christen** glauben an Jesus Christus.

1 Word pairs

Welche Wörter passen zusammen?

carriage
a crime
fruit
hair
lover
river
space
wet

1) become
2) commit
3) canned
4) create
5) crowded
6) polluted
7) secret
8) shiny

New words ▸ pp. 77 – 78

The USA is a strong military ____________.	Die USA sind eine starke Militär**macht**.
My bank gives me good ________________ advice.	Meine Bank gibt mir gute **finanzielle** Ratschläge.
People from India are called ____________.	Menschen aus Indien nennt man **Inder**.
It's so hot – turn the ____________________ on!	Es ist so heiß – schalte die **Klimaanlage** ein!
Such hats were ____________ of the 18th century.	Solche Hüte waren **typisch** für das 18. Jahrhundert.
The story of Robin Hood is a __________.	Die Geschichte von Robin Hood ist eine **Legende**.
Canadian forests are ______________ in autumn.	Kanadische Wälder sind **farbenprächtig** im Herbst.
Eddie went to the party in his gorilla __________.	Eddie ging in seinem Gorilla**kostüm** zur Party.
He's one of the teachers __________ lessons I like.	Er ist einer der Lehrer, **dessen** Unterricht ich mag.
Her relationship was full of love and __________.	Ihre Beziehung war voller Liebe und **Leidenschaft**.
His new monitor has a 21-inch __________.	Sein neuer Monitor hat einen 21-Zoll **Bildschirm**.
For many people, death is a __________ topic.	Für viele Leute ist der Tod ein **Tabu**thema.

2 Words with a similar meaning

Finde Wörter, die das Gleiche bedeuten wie die fettgedruckten Wörter.
Trage sie ein und schreibe die deutsche Übersetzung auf.

1	There's an **old story** / legend about this Scottish castle.	Legende, Sage
2	The air conditioning cost **almost** / ________________ £2,000!	________________
3	There's not enough **room** / ________________ in the garage for the bike.	________________
4	We hoped he would **come back** / ________________, but he never did.	________________
5	It took a while, but **in the end** / ________________ he told me everything.	________________
6	The carriage was so **full** / ________________ – I could hardly get on.	________________
7	Tomorrow we will **go on** / ________________ with our lesson.	________________
8	I often go to India – I was in Mumbai **not long ago** / ________________.	________________
9	Don't forget to **enclose** / ________________ your CV.	________________
10	I don't have the **energy** / ________________ to run a marathon.	________________
11	You can't swim in this river – it's too **dirty** / ________________.	________________
12	My computer is OK, but I need a new **monitor** / ________________.	________________

New words ► p. 79

A ________ travels to work every day.	Ein **Pendler** fährt jeden Tag zur Arbeit.
You can drive very fast on the M6 ________.	Man kann auf der **Autobahn** M6 sehr schnell fahren.
Wimbledon is a ________ of London.	Wimbledon ist ein **Vorort** von London.
That dress looks lovely – very ________!	Das Kleid sieht toll aus – sehr **schick**!
I often feel ________ – I have so much to do.	Ich fühle mich oft **gestresst** – ich habe so viel zu tun.
Too much ________ in life makes you ill.	Zuviel **Stress** im Leben macht krank.

3 Definitions

Vervollständige die Definitionen mit Wörtern aus dem Laptop-Monitor.
Trage die richtige Lösung von den USB-Sticks in die rechte Spalte ein.

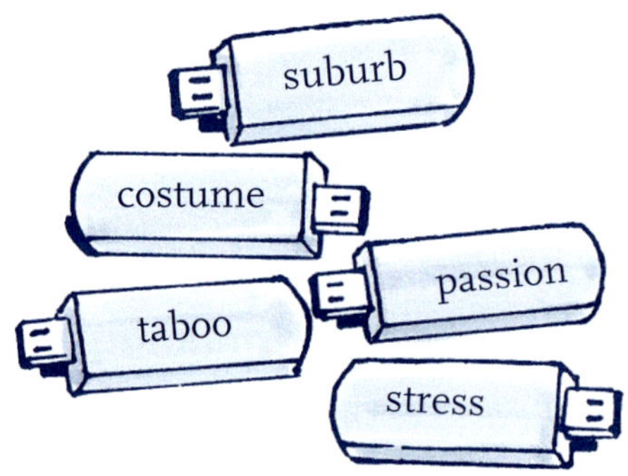

1 bad feeling or ________ caused by problems or too much ________ ________

2 the ________ an actor wears when he plays a particular ________ ________

3 a general ________ not to do or say a particular ________ ________

4 an ________ where people live that is outside the ________ of a city ________

5 a very strong ________ of ________ ________

4 Odd word out

Ein Wort passt nicht.
Finde und unterstreiche es.

1 Hindu – Indian – Muslim – Christian

2 colourful – financial – shiny – bright

3 railway – motorway – road – street

4 donate – give – lend – reach out

5 cinema – film – taboo – screen

6 whole – who – whose – which

7 bill – coin – note – space

8 fancy – turtle – lover – passion

New words ▸ *p. 80*

It's the poorest ________________ in New York.	Es ist die ärmste **Gegend** in New York.
What kind of jeans – __________ or tight?	Was für eine Jeans – **weit** oder eng?
The Queen doesn't have much __________ power.	Die Queen hat nicht viel **politische** Macht.
He spent one night in a prison __________.	Er verbrachte eine Nacht in einer Gefängnis**zelle**.
Rappers use a lot of ________ in their texts.	Rapper verwenden viel **Slang** in ihren Texten.
She only has clothes with a designer _________.	Sie hat nur Kleider mit einem Designer-**Etikett**.
Paul and Sue are a __________ without children.	Paul and Sue sind ein **Paar** ohne Kinder.
I'm ____________________ – is it red or green?	Ich bin **farbenblind** – ist es rot oder grün?
Operas and concerts are _____________ events.	Opern und Konzerte sind **kulturelle** Veranstaltungen.

5 Crossword

Trage die Übersetzungen der deutschen Wörter ins Rätsel ein.

Across
(2) farbenfroh
(5) Zelle
(7) Spannung
(10) Viertel / Nachbarschaft
(13) finanziell
(15) Paar
(16) verursachen
(17) Christ/in
(18) weit geschnitten
(19) kulturell

Down
(1) Leidenschaft
(2) Klarstellung
(3) Marke / Etikett
(4) Quittung
(6) Vorort
(8) ermutigen / fördern
(9) vor kurzem / in der letzten Zeit
(11) Möglichkeit, Gelegenheit
(12) politisch
(14) Pendler/in

New words ▸ p. 81

Apartheid was __________ discrimination.	Apartheid war **Rassen**diskriminierung.
He lost his job because of the __________ situation.	Er verlor seinen Job wegen der **Wirtschaftslage**.
Many poor countries have a high birth __________.	Viele arme Länder haben eine hohe Geburten**rate**.
It's only a fan website, not the __________ one.	Es ist nur eine Fan-Webseite, nicht die **offizielle**.
The writer has written many __________.	Der Schriftsteller hat viele **Romane** geschrieben.
The house was __________ by the police.	Das Haus war von der Polizei **umstellt**.

6 Lost words

Ergänze die Sätze mit der jeweils korrekten Präposition.

1 There were too many passengers __________ the train.

2 The carriage was crowded __________ people.

3 Tom will be late again – that's typical __________ him!

4 The temperature has gone up __________ ten per cent.

5 John has just too much stress __________ work at the moment.

6 I think more people should donate money __________ charity.

7 There are some very nice people __________ our neighbourhood.

8 We should protest __________ racial discrimination.

9 There were only a couple __________ men in the pub.

10 The instructions __________ the label say you can't wash the jacket.

11 He reached out __________ the book, but the shelf was too high.

12 Hold on __________ my arm, Granny – I'll help you to walk.

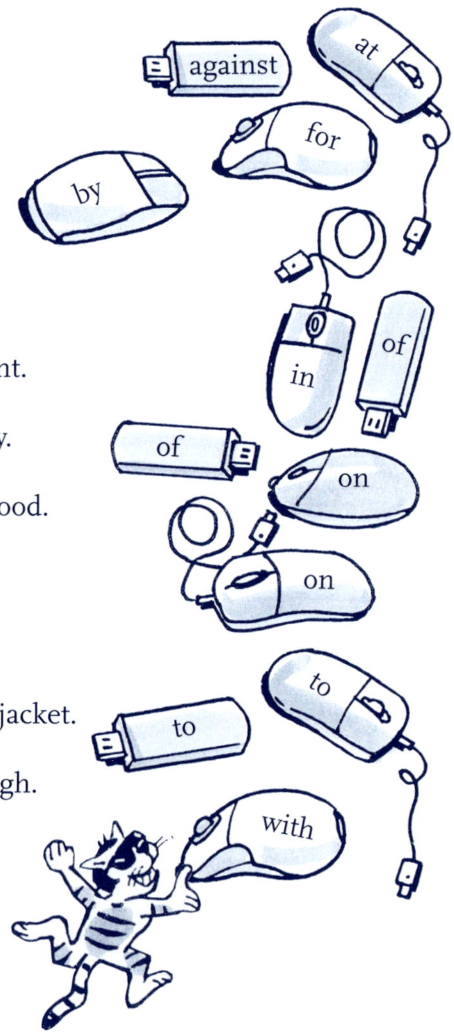

7 The fourth word

Welches Wort fehlt hier?

1	sun – dry	rain – __________	5	crowd – crowded	can – __________
2	BE – rubbish	AE – __________	6	culture – cultural	race – __________
3	land – tortoise	water – __________	7	school – classroom	prison – __________
4	car – mechanic	computer – __________	8	8-year-old – child	30-year-old – __________

New words ▸ p. 82

After a long war there was finally ___________.	Nach einem langen Krieg gab es endlich **Frieden.**
He feels ______________ when you talk about sex.	Er ist **verlegen**, wenn man über Sex spricht.
Here we are – ____________________ I was born.	Da wären wir – **hier** wurde ich geboren.
The soldier took his gun and __________ him.	Der Soldat nahm seine Waffe und **erschoss** ihn.
They were killed in the Soweto _______________.	Sie wurden im Soweto-**Aufstand** getötet.
The new shoes were in a _______________ box.	Die neuen Schuhe waren in einem **Papp**karton.
Gold is a valuable __________.	Gold ist ein wertvolles **Metall.**
Please __________ me to buy some eggs.	Bitte **erinnere** mich **daran**, Eier zu kaufen.
The outside is hard, but the __________ is soft.	Das Äußere ist hart, aber das **Innere** ist weich.
Nobody said anything – everyone was __________.	Niemand sagte etwas – alle waren **still.**
Please __________ your jacket in your wardrobe.	**Häng** deine Jacke bitte in deinen Kleiderschrank.
I __________ my father was still alive.	Ich **wünschte** mein Vater lebte noch.
I don't like saunas – I can't __________ the heat.	Saunas mag ich nicht – ich **ertrage** die Hitze nicht.
He wanted to sleep, but ____________ he couldn't.	Er wollte schlafen, aber **irgendwie** konnte er nicht.

8 Opposites

Trage das Gegenteil der fettgedruckten Wörter in die Lücken ein.

1 **healthy** / _____________ lifestyle
2 feel quite **relaxed** / _____________
3 **agree** / _____________ with somebody
4 a **noisy** / _____________ street
5 live in **the centre** / a _____________ of a city
6 look from the **outside** / _____________
7 a **wanted** / an _____________ child
8 **war** / _____________ between two countries
9 a **crowded** / an _____________ room
10 wear **old-fashioned** / _____________ clothes
11 be **tolerant** / _____________
12 do **well** / _____________ in a test
13 be **single** / _____________
14 suddenly **appear** / _____________
15 **true** / _____________ information
16 **buy** / _____________ a car
17 wear **tight** / _____________ jeans
18 the **best** / _____________ novel
19 become **wet** / _____________
20 a **clean** / _____________ river

New words ▸pp. 83–85

Everybody was silent to ____________ the victims.	Alle waren still, um der Opfer zu **gedenken.**
Thank you for your __________ about our courses.	Vielen Dank für Ihre **Anfrage** zu unseren Kursen.
I'd like to __________ about the tickets.	Ich möchte **mich** nach den Fahrkarten **erkundigen.**
Is this your own flat or do you __________ it?	Ist das deine Wohnung oder **mietest** du sie?
Spam e-mails often have strange ______________.	Spam-Emails haben oft komische **Betreffzeilen.**

9 Two-part verbs

Vervollständige die Sätze mit einem passenden Wort von den USB-Sticks.

1 He reached ____________ for the book, but the shelf was too high.

2 Hold ____________ to my arm, Granny – I'll help you to walk.

3 What a mess! Now straighten ____________ your room immediately!

4 Don't worry – things will work ____________ in the end.

5 She cried for help, but people just walked ____________.

6 Come on, try again! Just don't give ____________!

7 He tore ____________ a piece of paper to write down her number.

8 Sorry, no tickets anymore. The concert is sold ____________.

9 She went ____________ to a policeman and asked for the way.

10 We were completely cut ____________ from the outside world.

10 Making new words

Bilde aus den Buchstaben des Wortes so viele neue Wörter wie möglich.
30 Wörter sollte man leicht finden, aber wer findet über 50?

date, cream,

New words ▸pp. 86–87

A tunnel ____________ England with France.	Ein Tunnel **verbindet** England mit Frankreich.
He walked through the ________ into the garden.	Er ging durch die **Pforte** in den Garten.
You can find all the sights in the ____________.	Alle Sehenswürdigkeiten findet man im **Reiseführer**.
In a ____________ country, the people can vote.	In einem **demokratischen** Land darf man wählen.
GDR stands for 'German Democratic ________'.	DDR steht für „Deutsche Demokratische **Republik**".
Our car was checked at the border ____________.	Unser Auto wurde am **Grenzübergang** durchsucht.
Please cross the road at the ________________!	Bitte überquere die Straße am **Überweg**!
In 1945 Berlin was divided into four __________.	1945 wurde Berlin in vier **Sektoren** aufgeteilt.
German ______________________ was in 1990.	Die deutsche **Wiedervereinigung** war 1990.
Should the two Koreas __________?	Sollten sich die beiden Koreas **wiedervereinigen**?
I don't like driving – I ________ taking the train.	Auto fahren mag ich nicht – ich fahre **lieber** Zug.
An ____________ designs houses and buildings.	Ein **Architekt** entwirft Häuser und Gebäude.

11 Word building

Verbinde die Wörter 1–14 mit jeweils einem passenden Wort aus der Mauer. Achte dabei auf die Schreibweise (getrennt oder zusammen), und trage die deutsche Übersetzung ein.

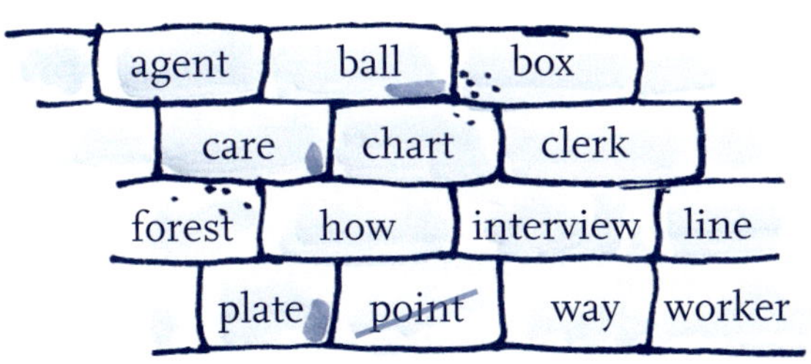

1	check point	____________	*8*	child ________	____________
2	subject ________	____________	*9*	bank ________	____________
3	travel ________	____________	*10*	rain ________	____________
4	motor ________	____________	*11*	mail ________	____________
5	social ________	____________	*12*	foot ________	____________
6	number ________	____________	*13*	job ________	____________
7	some ________	____________	*14*	pie ________	____________

New words ▸p. 88

Cleaning your teeth daily __________ toothache.	Tägliches Zähneputzen **verhindert** Zahnschmerzen.
Turn the light off – it only __________ insects.	Mach das Licht aus – es **zieht** nur Insekten **an**.
Parliament is a political __________________.	Das Parlament ist eine politische **Einrichtung**.
__________ is very important for our hotels.	Der **Tourismus** ist sehr wichtig für unsere Hotels.
He put a ___________ on the overhead projector.	Er legte eine **Folie** auf den Overhead-Projektor.
She practised her _________ in front of a mirror.	Sie übte ihren **Vortrag** vor dem Spiegel.
A student _______________ on the environment.	Ein Schüler **hielt einen Vortrag** über die Umwelt.
There was a large screen, but no _____________.	Es gab eine große Leinwand, aber keinen **Beamer**.
The lights created amazing __________ effects.	Die Lichter erzeugten erstaunliche **optische** Effekte.
What __________ is the shirt made of? – Cotton.	Aus welchem **Material** ist das Hemd? – Baumwolle.

12 Word families

a) Finde die passenden Verben zu den angegebenen Nomen.

1 reunification – ____________	*6* talk – ____________	*11* advice – ____________
2 application – ____________	*7* shot – ____________	*12* crossing – ____________
3 introduction – ____________	*8* need – ____________	*13* decision – ____________
4 attraction – ____________	*9* belief – ____________	*14* enquiry – ____________
5 advertisement – ____________	*10* use – ____________	*15* reaction – ____________

b) Vervollständige die Sätze mit der korrekten Form eines Verbs oder Nomens aus a).

1 Stop! It's not safe to _______________ the road here.

2 Everybody in our class has to give a(n) _______________ on their favourite hobby.

3 Did you see the advertisement? If I were you, I would _______________ for the job.

4 Life has changed for lots of people since German _______________.

5 I sent off a(n) _______________, but the information I received was useless.

6 Well, I would _______________ you to change jobs.

New words ▸pp. 89–90

The hotel ____________ gave us the key.	Die Hotel-**Empfangsdame** gab uns den Schlüssel.
You can now ________ for your flight.	Sie können sich jetzt für Ihren Flug **einchecken**.
Does the price of the room ______ breakfast?	Ist das Frühstück im Zimmerpreis **enthalten**?
I have a ____________ for two tickets.	Ich habe eine **Reservierung** für zwei Karten.
I'll ______ a table at the Chinese restaurant.	Ich **reserviere** einen Tisch im Chinarestaurant.
We slept in the large _________ of a hostel.	Wir schliefen im großen **Schlafsaal** einer Herberge.
The city was _________ after the war.	Die Stadt wurde nach dem Krieg **wieder aufgebaut**.
The coach didn't want to ______ on the match.	Der Trainer wollte sich nicht zum Spiel **äußern**.
The smell _____ her ________ to the gas.	Der Geruch machte sie auf das Gas **aufmerksam**.
Please _________ to contact us at any time.	Sie **können** uns **gerne** jederzeit kontaktieren.
We saw a ______-show about Australia.	Wir sahen eine **Dia**show über Australien.

13 Word groups

Ordne den drei Oberbegriffen auf den Laptops jeweils sechs passende Wörter zu.
Weitere sechs Wörter aus der Box passen zu keinem der Oberbegriffe.

~~(to) book~~ – breakfast – cardboard – carriage – cell – commuter – crowded – dormitory – institution – key card – legend – passenger – projector – railway – receptionist – reservation – rush hour – screen – sector – slide – talk – transparency – uprising – visual

14 Spot the mistakes

In jedem Satz sind zwei Fehler. Unterstreiche und korrigiere sie.

1 The president don't want to comment the economic situation. ______ ______

2 Woman often wear a costume for a job interview. ______ ______

3 I couldn't gave my talk – the beamer was broken. ______ ______

4 I wish I have a room with an air conditioning in this heat. ______ ______

5 John, can I remember you to enquire for a hotel room? ______ ______

6 I would have ask her out, but I was too embarassed. ______ ______

15 Verb forms

Ergänze die Tabelle der unregelmäßigen Verben.

1	take	took	taken
2		drew	
3	catch		
4		held	
5	rebuild		
6			drunk

7			hung
8	let		
9		stood	
10			risen
11	teach		
12		shot	

16 Word stress

Unterstreiche bei allen Wörtern die Silbe, die betont werden muss.

architect	attraction	candidate	chemistry
credit card	cultural	fashionable	financial
institution	legend	material	metal
military	Muslim	official	passenger
passion	physics	popular	republic
social	tourism	vandalism	visual

17 Word search: Big city life

Finde 30 Begriffe aus dem Wortfeld „Leben in der Großstadt“. (↓ →) Übersetze sie ins Deutsche.

S	F	E	Z	X	W	S	L	B	Z	D	Z	W	U	O	U	H	L	N	P
Q	F	H	Z	H	T	Z	A	I	R	P	O	R	T	U	B	U	S	T	K
U	T	R	S	T	A	T	I	O	N	O	L	B	O	D	P	L	T	S	T
A	S	N	M	X	M	D	Z	W	D	D	X	S	U	M	C	R	R	A	Z
R	E	S	T	A	U	R	A	N	T	J	W	L	R	M	X	L	A	G	F
E	K	Q	Y	P	Y	F	C	F	O	G	C	U	I	A	W	I	F	R	I
J	B	O	T	T	W	H	O	T	E	L	V	M	S	L	A	R	F	A	I
N	E	I	G	H	B	O	U	R	H	O	O	D	M	L	Q	N	I	F	T
T	H	E	A	T	R	E	I	F	I	S	T	A	D	I	U	M	C	F	W
S	D	H	T	U	N	D	E	R	G	R	O	U	N	D	O	E	G	I	B
S	K	Y	S	C	R	A	P	E	R	J	F	A	C	T	O	R	Y	T	U
Y	S	E	L	O	F	F	I	C	E	U	U	N	G	N	L	B	L	I	I
X	T	X	U	Z	E	A	C	O	T	R	A	I	N	S	C	L	F	C	Z
T	X	N	F	S	R	Q	N	M	R	W	U	M	O	T	O	R	W	A	Y
R	B	I	S	P	A	V	E	M	E	N	T	V	C	O	N	C	E	R	T
A	H	V	P	P	I	H	O	U	X	C	Q	D	T	S	K	N	J	R	B
M	S	S	E	V	L	N	M	T	H	L	E	W	X	B	Z	K	Z	I	C
K	Z	J	G	T	W	A	Q	E	S	U	B	U	R	B	H	Q	V	A	U
N	U	E	A	K	A	W	X	R	E	B	I	I	N	T	A	X	I	G	V
X	Y	I	R	U	Y	I	N	D	U	S	T	R	Y	X	U	K	Z	E	C

airport – Flughafen

New words ▸ p. 6

She's so __________ – I liked her immediately.	Sie ist so **charmant** – ich mochte sie sofort.
It's __________ to think you're something better.	Es ist **arrogant**, sich für etwas Besseres zu halten.
She always stayed __________ to her boss.	Sie blieb ihrem Chef gegenüber immer **loyal**.
He's always nervous – he has no __________.	Er ist immer nervös – er hat kein **Selbstvertrauen**.
She looks __________ in that beautiful dress.	Sie sieht in dem schönen Kleid **attraktiv** aus.
The big glasses makes her __________.	Die große Brille macht sie **unattraktiv**.
A beard and glasses change your __________.	Bart und Brille verändern dein **Aussehen**.
He didn't even __________ I had a new dress on!	Er **merkte** nicht mal, dass ich ein neues Kleid trug!
Her hair was long, blond and __________.	Ihr Haar war lang, blond und **lockig**.
His hair was curly, not __________.	Sein Haar war lockig, nicht **glatt**.
He's funny – I like his __________.	Er ist lustig – ich mag seinen **Sinn für Humor**.
__________ with salt are the best nuts.	**Erdnüsse** mit Salz sind die besten Nüsse.
Spain is always sunny, __________ Ireland.	Spanien ist immer sonnig, **im Gegensatz zu** Irland.

1 The best word

Finde das Wort A, B, C oder D, das am besten in die Lücke passt.

A find, B notice, C nod, D attract	1 Did you __________ her hair? It's curly now.
A drop, B draw, C dress, D drive	2 Let me __________ your attention to this bar chart.
A loyal, B political, C visual, D official	3 Whatever happens, we will be __________ to the king!
A reunify, B enquire, C rebuild, D include	4 Does the DVD __________ extra material?
A present, B prefer, C prevent, D rent	5 We need to __________ another accident like this!
A apprentice, B appointment, C application, D appearance	6 Her dog had the __________ of a wolf.

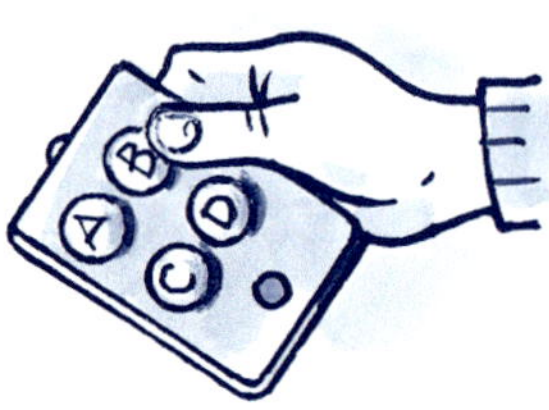

New words ▸ p. 7

We like him – he's strange but ____________.	Wir mögen ihn – er ist seltsam, aber **liebenswert**.
The ice is too ________ to walk on.	Das Eis ist zu **dünn**, um darauf zu laufen.
Put on a __________ pullover – it's very cold!	Zieh einen **dicken** Pullover an – es ist sehr kalt!
She smiled ______ a friendly ________.	Sie lächelte **auf** freundliche **Art und Weise**.
'Nice dress!' is a simple _________________.	„Schönes Kleid!" ist ein einfacher **Anmachspruch**.
I fancy him – how can I ________ him _____?	Ich steh auf ihn – wie kann ich ihn **anquatschen**?

2 Crossword

Trage die Übersetzungen der deutschen Wörter ins Rätsel ein.

Across
(1) Aussehen, Erscheinung
(3) charmant
(5) Schlafsaal
(7) anstrengend, stressig
(9) Roman
(10) verursachen
(14) liebenswert
(15) lagern
(16) deren, dessen

Down
(2) Selbstvertrauen/ Zuversicht
(3) (er)schaffen
(4) trocken
(6) Dia/Folie
(7) geeignet, passend
(8) lautlos/schweigend
(11) anders als
(12) reagieren
(13) (ver)trauen

3 Odd word out

Ein Wort passt nicht.
Finde und unterstreiche es.

1 talk – chat – speak – draw
2 thin – large – huge – big
3 curly – social – straight – shiny
4 baggy – tight – torn – racial
5 peanut – apple – banana – orange
6 transparency – slide – gate – projector
7 lovable – arrogant – charming – nice
8 (to) book – reception – checkpoint – check in

New words ▸ p. 8

This film is a ________________ story.	Die Filmhandlung ist **aus dem wirklichen Leben**.
She hates maths, and I don't like it ____________ .	Sie hasst Mathe, und ich mag es **auch** nicht.
I don't know where he is – ____________ he's ill.	Ich weiß nicht, wo er ist – **vielleicht** ist er krank.
I found myself in a difficult ________________ .	Ich befand mich in einer schwierigen **Lage**.
He won't give you his bike? That's ____________ !	Er gibt dir nicht sein Fahrrad? Das ist **gemein**!

4 Lost words

Ergänze die Sätze mit der jeweils korrekten Präposition. Bei einem der Sätze bleibt die Lücke leer.

1 He didn't want to comment ________________ the new situation.

2 The garden was surrounded ________________ a tall wall.

3 She's so funny – I like her sense ________________ humour!

4 Can you lend ________________ me £10?

5 He's quite tall ________________ a boy of his age.

6 Can you perhaps explain it ________________ a different way?

7 Good friends are usually loyal ________________ each other.

8 He should care more ________________ his appearance.

9 Oh, I didn't notice you were ________________ the party.

10 A motorway connects the airport ________________ the city.

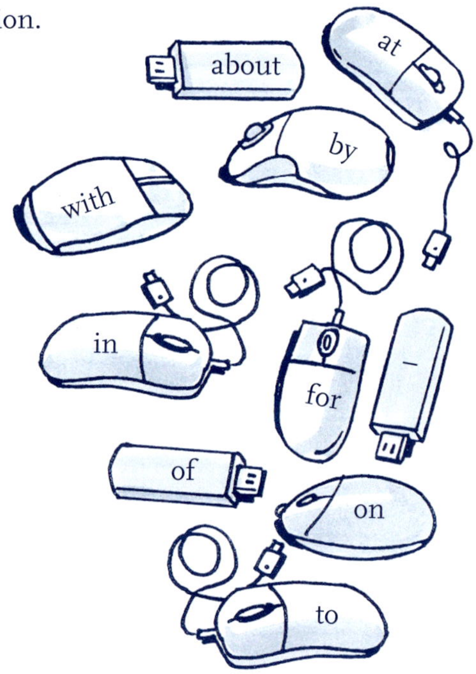

5 What are the words?

Wie übersetzt man die fettgedruckten Wörter ins Deutsche?

1 We were on our **way** to London. ________________

2 They served us in a friendly **way**. ________________

3 I think we're going the wrong **way**. ________________

4 There's a mistake in **line** two of the article. ________________

5 I can't think of a good chat-up **line**. ________________

6 I'm sorry, but Mr Jones is talking on the other **line**. ________________

7 Which underground **line** goes to the airport? ________________

New words ▸ p. 9

Why did she ____________ with her boyfriend?	Warum hat sie **sich** von ihrem Freund **getrennt**?
It didn't work out – I __________ things ______!	Es hat nicht geklappt – ich habe **alles vermasselt**!
Cheap shoes never __________ very long.	Billige Schuhe **halten** nie sehr lange.
Please tell me ____________ you can come or not.	Bitte sag mir, **ob** du kommen kannst oder nicht.
I hate it when you __________ with other boys!	Ich hasse es, wenn du mit anderen Jungen **flirtest**!
So you love her – ______________________ her?	Du liebst sie also – **warum sagst** du es ihr **nicht**?

6 Two-part verbs

Vervollständige die Sätze mit einem passenden Wort von den USB-Sticks.

1 I feel bad – I think I always mess things ______________.

2 Come ______________! It's time to go now.

3 She broke ______________ with Dan last week.

4 He got ______________ the bus and ran away.

5 Now she's going ______________ with Jo.

6 She chatted him ______________ at a disco.

7 Then he asked her ______________ for a pizza.

8 I put ______________ my glasses to read the menu.

9 At the weekend I hang ______________ with my friends.

10 When the police arrived, he took ______________ in a fast car.

7 Making new words

Bilde aus den Buchstaben des Wortes so viele neue Wörter wie möglich. Wenn du zehn Wörter findest: nicht schlecht. 15 Wörter: sehr gut. 20 oder mehr Wörter: absolute Spitze!

act, ice,

attractive

New words ▸ pp. 10–11

He kissed her on her full, red ____________.	Er küsste sie auf ihre vollen, roten **Lippen**.
She should work harder – she's too ____________.	Sie sollte härter arbeiten – sie ist zu **faul**.
He ____________ her name four of five times.	Er **erwähnte** ihren Namen vier oder fünf Mal.
The DJ tried to ____________ the party ____________.	Der DJ versuchte, die Party **in Gang** zu **halten**.
Sorry, I didn't ____________ your name.	Ich habe Ihren Namen leider nicht **verstanden**.
It's the best restaurant ____________ here.	Es ist das beste Restaurant hier **in der Gegend**.

8 Verb forms

Ergänze die Tabelle der unregelmäßigen Verben.

1	go	went	gone
2		hit	
3	catch		
4		kept	
5	break		

6			rung
7	leave		
8		sold	
9			stolen
10	fight		

9 Pronunciation

Ordne die Wörter der richtigen Aussprachegruppe zu,
je nachdem, wie der unterstrichene Vokal ausgesprochen wird.

æ	ɑː	eɪ	ə
arrogant (1)			

charming, last, label, loyal, perhaps, attractive (1), racial, ask, catch, lazy, arrogant (2), around, shame, hand, attractive (2), command, ~~arrogant (1)~~, calm, nature, lovable

New words ▸ *p. 12 (part 1)*

A candlelight dinner is very ________________.	Abendessen bei Kerzenlicht ist sehr **romantisch**.
She seemed OK, but ______________ she was ill.	Sie wirkte OK, aber in **Wirklichkeit** war sie krank.
Your boyfriend is arrogant – just __________ him!	Dein Freund ist arrogant – **mach Schluss** mit ihm!
The story of *Star Trek* is __________ in the future.	Die Handlung von *Star Trek* **spielt** in der Zukunft.
Who ________________ the first *Twilight* film?	Wer hat beim ersten *Twilight*-Film **Regie geführt**?
Steven Spielberg is a famous ________________.	Steven Spielberg ist ein berühmter **Regisseur**.
Troy __________ Brad Pitt as Achilles.	*Troja* **hat** Brad Pitt als Achilles **in der Hauptrolle**.
He studied __________ and now works in court.	Er hat **Jura** studiert und arbeitet jetzt am Gericht.
The immigrant became a victim of ____________.	Der Einwanderer wurde ein Opfer von **Rassismus**.
Lord of the Rings is a great ______________ film.	*Herr der Ringe* ist ein toller **Fantasy**-Film.
The film is __________ on a true story.	Der Film **basiert** auf einer wahren Geschichte.

10 Word pairs

Welche Wörter passen am besten zusammen?

1) (to) direct
2) (to) dump
3) (to) earn
4) (to) eat
5) (to) last
6) (to) notice
7) (to) return
8) (to) stress
9) (to) study
10) (to) wear

a boyfriend
a film
forever
home
law
a mistake
money
a peanut
a shirt
a syllable

New words ▸ p. 12 (part 2)

______________ I can't go to the party.	**Leider** kann ich nicht zur Party gehen.
____________ nobody died in the accident.	**Zum Glück** starb niemand bei dem Unfall.
Dracula is a famous ____________.	Dracula ist ein berühmter **Vampir**.
She became __________ and had her first child.	Sie wurde **schwanger** und bekam ihr erstes Kind.
He lost __________ of his car on the ice.	Auf dem Eis verlor er die **Kontrolle** über sein Auto.
Pit bulls are dangerous because they _________.	Pitbulls sind gefährlich, weil sie **beißen**.
The film's ____________________ look so real!	Die **Spezialeffekte** des Films sehen so echt aus!
She began to feel the __________ of the alcohol.	Sie begann die **Wirkung** des Alkohols zu spüren.
Most of the film ____________ were positive.	Die meisten **Kritiken** des Films waren positiv.
New films are often ___________ in the paper.	Neue Filme werden oft in der Zeitung **rezensiert**.
He works as a book ___________ for *The Times*.	Er arbeitet als Buch**kritiker** für die *Times*.

11 Word friends

Auf jedem Plakat gibt es vier Wörter/Wortverbindungen, die direkt nach dem Verb auf dem kleinen Zettel folgen können. Unterstreiche sie.

New words ▸ p. 13

Nine ____________ ten people didn't know the film.	Neun **von** zehn Leuten kannten den Film nicht.
In Christian ______________ there is only one God.	In der christlichen **Religion** gibt es nur einen Gott.
Is there ________________ life on other planets?	Gibt es **intelligentes** Leben auf anderen Planeten?
I'll do it as soon as possible – just be ____________!	Ich mache es so bald wie möglich – sei **geduldig**!
Give her more time – you're too ________________.	Gib ihr mehr Zeit – du bist zu **ungeduldig**.
That's very ____________ of you to help me.	Das ist sehr **freundlich** von dir, mir zu helfen.

12 Words with different meanings

Finde auf der Liste (Seestern-Magnet) ein passendes Wort zu den beiden Sätzen/Satzteilen auf den Zetteln 1 – 9. Trage es dort ein und unterstreiche die beiden deutschen Entsprechungen.

1)
a) Er schaute sie auf seltsame Art und Weise an.
b) Wir gehen in die falsche Richtung!
way

2)
a) Das ist gegen das Gesetz!
b) Nach der Schule will sie Jura studieren.
____

3)
a) Letzte Woche war ich im Kino.
b) Diese Schuhe werden nicht lange halten.
____

direct
kind
last
law
mean
notice
set
straight
~~way~~

4)
a) Sie will dem Mörder eine Falle stellen.
b) Der Film spielt in Australien.
____

5)
a) Du wirst keinen Unterschied merken.
b) Was steht da auf dem Aushang?
____

6)
a) Sie müssen immer geradeaus gehen.
b) Ihre Haare waren lang und glatt.
____

7)
a) Was für eine Art von Musik machen sie?
b) Das war wirklich nett von dir!
____

8)
a) Er wollte bei dem Film nicht Regie führen.
b) Direkte Fragen können unhöflich wirken.
____

9)
a) Was kann das nur bedeuten?
b) Dein Bruder ist aber gemein!
____

New words ▸ *p. 14*

Fantastic! What a ____________ idea!	Fantastisch! Was für eine **glänzende** Idee!
Landing on the moon was a ____________ event.	Die Mondlandung war ein **historisches** Ereignis.
He saw the old photo and became ____________.	Er sah das alte Foto und wurde **sentimental**.
Is there a restaurant that you can ____________?	Gibt es ein Restaurant, das du **empfehlen** kannst?
The film won a lot of international ____________.	Der Film hat viele internationale **Preise** gewonnen.

13 Opposites

Trage das Gegenteil der fettgedruckten Wörter in die Lücken ein.

1 have **straight** / ____________ hair

2 an **intelligent** / a ____________ person

3 **fortunately** / ____________

4 a **hard-working** / ____________ student

5 a **thin** / ____________ book

6 a **thin** / ____________ cat

7 he's **like** / ____________ his brother

8 an **attractive** / ____________ girl

9 a **patient** / an ____________ child

10 **forget** / ____________ someone's birthday

14 Scrambled words: Personality and character

Die Buchstaben auf der linken Seite der Anzeigetafel ergeben Wörter, die die menschliche Persönlichkeit beschreiben. Trage die gefundenen Wörter in die mittlere Spalte der Tafel ein. Die Tipps helfen dir.

			TIP
1	DINK		you're nice
2	ZAYL		you don't like working
3	NAME		you're not nice to others
4	ALLOY		you always support friends
5	TRAGNORA		you think you're fantastic
6	COMATRIN		you show your feelings of love
7	TIPNEAT		you don't mind waiting
8	GIINNLLEETT		you're clever

New words ▸ p. 15

I never have any ideas – I'm not very ___.	Ich habe nie Ideen – ich bin nicht sehr **kreativ**.
He lost his ___ on the fastest horse.	Er verlor seine **Wette** auf das schnellste Pferd.
Have you got a car? And ___, what kind?	Hast du ein Auto? Und **wenn ja**, was für eins?
A mayor is active in local ___.	Ein Bürgermeister ist in der Lokal**politik** aktiv.
We should do more to save the ___.	Wir sollten mehr tun, um die **Umwelt** zu retten.

15 Word search: Films

Finde 20 Begriffe aus dem Wortfeld „Film" und übersetze sie ins Deutsche. (↓ →)

T	E	R	C	T	O	D	S	O	U	N	D	T	R	A	C	K	A
N	O	S	R	R	S	C	R	E	E	N	E	A	O	M	H	R	A
D	T	S	M	O	V	I	E	S	E	A	F	A	N	T	A	S	Y
H	E	T	C	R	S	N	V	T	A	W	C	A	M	E	R	A	R
S	C	I	C	A	U	E	I	U	M	A	O	I	S	T	A	R	R
C	E	T	S	C	O	M	E	D	Y	R	E	A	R	E	C	T	W
E	P	L	O	T	U	A	W	I	H	D	I	R	E	C	T	O	R
N	H	E	R	O	N	T	E	O	C	O	S	T	U	M	E	S	D
E	A	S	M	R	E	M	E	T	H	R	I	L	L	E	R	Y	A

soundtrack – Filmmusik

16 Words with a similar meaning

Finde Wörter, die das Gleiche bedeuten wie die fettgedruckten Wörter.
Trage sie ein und schreibe die deutsche Übersetzung auf.

1 When she spoke, everybody was **quiet** / silent . still

2 Where's the station? – Sorry, I'm not from **this area** / ______________ . ______________

3 She should really **break up with** / ______________ her boyfriend. ______________

4 Sara is quite beautiful – and **clever** / ______________ too. ______________

5 It was very **nice** / ______________ of him to drive me home. ______________

6 The Oscar is a famous film **prize** / ______________ . ______________

7 I don't know where she is – **maybe** / ______________ she's ill. ______________

8 It looks like a boring place, but **in fact** / ______________ it's great! ______________

9 We can't say **if** / ______________ it is true or not. ______________

10 I didn't **get** / ______________ your name – could you repeat it, please? ______________

17 Definitions

Vervollständige die Definitionen mit Wörtern von dem Laptop-Monitor.
Trage die richtige Lösung von den USB-Sticks in die rechte Spalte ein.

1 a dead person who attacks people at ______________ to drink their ______________ ______________

2 a ______________ that gives a personal ______________ about a new book or film ______________

3 someone who tells the ______________ in a film how to play a ______________ ______________

4 the red, soft ______________ of your body which is around the ______________ ______________

5 the belief of a ______________ of people in a ______________ ______________

6 a formal ______________ , like an ______________ , a Grammy, etc. ______________

18 The fourth word

Welches Wort fehlt hier?

1 attract – attractive	create – ______	*5* kiss – lips	bite – ______
2 Christian – church	Muslim – ______	*6* house – door	garden – ______
3 credit card – plastic	coin – ______	*7* politics – political	history – ______
4 reliable – character	beautiful – ______	*8* cardboard – thick	paper – ______

19 Word stress

Unterstreiche bei allen Wörtern die Silbe, die betont werden muss.

address	arrogant	attractive	brilliant
creative	effect	humour	ideal
intelligent	loyal	patient	politics
pregnant	religion	sentimental	situation
technology	unfortunately	unpopular	vampire

20 Spot the mistakes

In jedem Satz sind zwei Fehler. Unterstreiche und korrigiere sie.

1 The film plays Johnny Depp as the loveable geek. ______ ______

2 I can't say weather they catched the thief or not. ______ ______

3 If you eat too many food, you'll become thick. ______ ______

4 His storys aren't very creative – he just has no fantasy! ______ ______

5 The film, which is basing on a real-life story, is setted in Italy. ______ ______

6 It wont snow, and it won't rain too. ______ ______

7 We're friends for 12 years now, so I know her quite good. ______ ______

8 The train is to expensive – I'd recommend to go by bus. ______ ______

B 6 Unit 2

New words ▸ p. 28

The flat's warm – it has central ____________.	Die Wohnung ist warm – sie hat Zentral**heizung**.
I don't like saunas – I can't stand the ________.	Saunas mag ich nicht – ich ertrage die **Hitze** nicht.
________ the oil and then add the onions.	**Erhitze** das Öl und füge dann die Zwiebeln hinzu.
________________ windows save energy.	Fenster mit **Doppelverglasung** sparen Energie.
I heat the water for my tea in the ________.	Ich erhitze mein Teewasser im **Wasserkocher**.
The new games ___________ is easier to use.	Die neue Spiel**konsole** ist leichter zu bedienen.
___________ of the house will save energy.	Die **Isolierung** des Hauses wird Energie sparen.
You can heat food quickly in a ___________.	Man kann Essen schnell in der **Mikrowelle** erhitzen.
Use the ______________ to change channels.	Nimm die **Fernbedienung** zum Umschalten.
Teachers need pens for the ______________.	Lehrer brauchen Stifte für das **Whiteboard**.
Our kitchen has lots of modern __________.	Unsere Küche hat jede Menge moderne **Apparate**.

1 Scrambled words: Technology

Die Buchstaben auf der linken Seite der Anzeigetafel ergeben Beispiele technischer Geräte. Trage die gefundenen Wörter in die mittlere Spalte der Tafel ein. Die Tipps helfen dir.

	✈ (departure)	✈ (arrival)	TIP
1	TELEKT		you heat water in it
2	LOSENOC		you play with it
3	INVITESOLE		you watch it
4	WARMVOICE		you heat food in it
5	DARTHBOWIE		you write on it
6	ODIVE TERROCOPJ		you show slides with it

New words ▸ p. 29 (part 1)

The CO_2 we produce is our ________________.	Unser CO_2-Ausstoß ist unsere **CO_2-Bilanz.**
Burning things produces ________________.	Durch Verbrennung entsteht **Kohlendioxid.**
A ____________ studies the sciences.	Ein **Wissenschaftler** studiert Naturwissenschaften.
Planes __________ CO_2 in the atmosphere.	Flugzeuge **setzen** CO_2 in die Atmosphäre **frei.**
He spends a large __________ of money on food.	Er gibt einen großen Geld**betrag** für Essen aus.
They never found the __________ of the fire.	Man hat nie die **Ursache** des Feuers gefunden.
CO_2 causes ________________.	CO_2 verursacht den **globalen Temperaturanstieg.**
Do your parents really __________ you to smoke?	**Erlauben** dir deine Eltern wirklich zu rauchen?

2 Crossword

Trage die Übersetzungen der deutschen Wörter ins Rätsel ein.

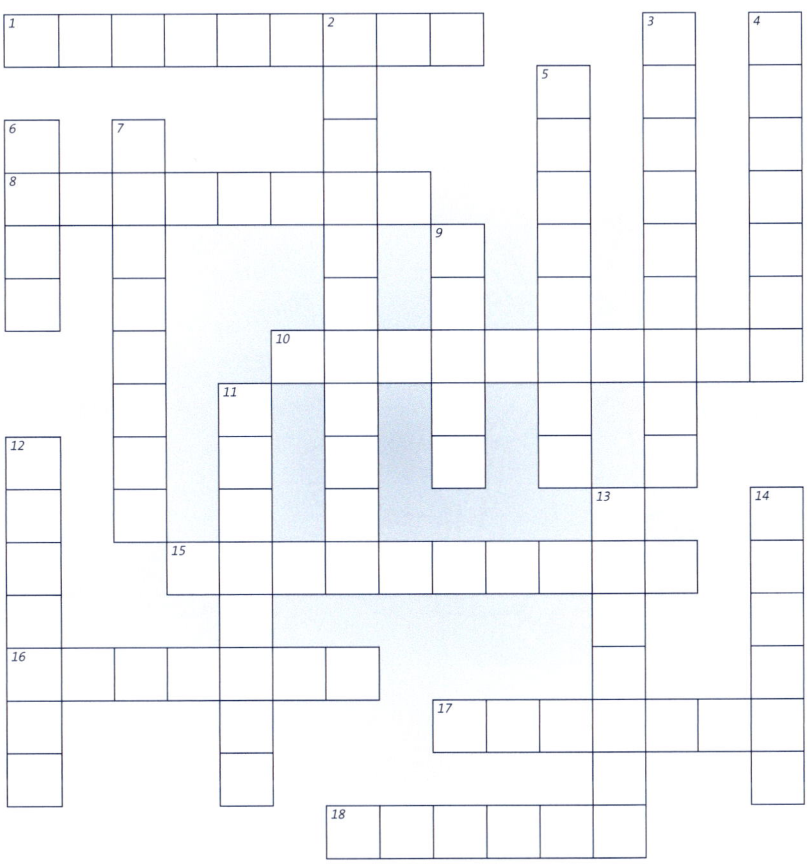

Across

(1) empfehlen
(8) Wirtschafts-, wirtschaftliche(r, s)
(10) Isolierung
(15) historisch
(16) Heizung
(17) freilassen, freisetzen
(18) Menge, Betrag

Down

(2) Umwelt/ Umgebung
(3) (Natur-)Wissen-schaftler/in
(4) erwähnen
(5) schwanger
(6) gemein
(7) verseucht, verunreinigt
(9) Ursache, Grund
(11) Politik
(12) ob
(13) geduldig
(14) (kleines) Gerät, Apparat

New words ▸ *p. 29 (part 2)*

The working ______ in the factory are bad.	Die Arbeits**bedingungen** in der Fabrik sind mies.
Dolphins can ______ with each other.	Delfine können miteinander **kommunizieren**.
Cars produce a lot of CO_2 ______.	Autos verursachen viele CO_2-**Emissionen**.
A ______ is a thousand kilograms.	Eine **Tonne** sind tausend Kilogramm.
Most of our body is ______ water.	Dar Großteil unseres Körpers **besteht aus** Wasser.
Electric ______ make life easier.	Elektro**geräte** erleichtern das Leben.
We've missed our sales ______ by 10%.	Wir haben unser Verkaufs**ziel** um 10% verfehlt.
The global ______ is getting warmer.	Das globale **Klima** wird wärmer.
Air is made up of different ______.	Luft besteht aus verschiedenen **Gasen**.

3 Definitions

Vervollständige die Definitionen mit Wörtern aus dem linken Display.
Trage die richtige Lösung aus dem anderen Display in die rechte Spalte ein.

1 the general weather ______ of a particular ______ ______

2 someone who does ______ in a field like biology or ______ ______

3 a ______ that is released by cars, ______, etc. ______

4 a ______ that helps you with your ______ at home ______

5 a system for producing hot ______ or air in a ______ ______

6 an ______ you try to hit, or a ______ you try to reach ______

New words ▸ p. 30

The wheel was the first great ____________.	Das Rad war die erste große **Erfindung**.
It __________ not be the best car, but I like it.	Es **mag** nicht das beste Auto sein, aber ich mag es.
Cars give people more ____________.	Autos geben den Menschen mehr **Mobilität**.
Wind __________ is a clean source of energy.	Wind**kraft** ist eine saubere Energiequelle.
Smoking can __________ to cancer.	Rauchen kann zu Krebs **führen**.
The French ____________ began in 1789.	Die Französische **Revolution** begann 1789.
__________ is black and burns well.	**Kohle** ist schwarz und brennt gut.
With the new __________, the car will start again.	Mit der neuen **Batterie** springt das Auto wieder an.
I had to do it – I had no __________.	Ich musste es tun – ich hatte keine **Wahl**.

4 Spot the mistakes

In jedem Satz sind zwei Fehler. Unterstreiche und korrigiere sie.

1 The earth's atmosphere is made up off different gasses. __________ __________

2 You need two sets of batterys for these games console. __________ __________

3 Our house has double glasses, so the rooms are very quite. __________ __________

4 Better insulation lead to less heat costs.. __________ __________

5 My parents are cool, but they don't allow me travelling allone. __________ __________

6 Carbon emissions is higher today as twenty years ago. __________ __________

5 Verb forms

Ergänze die Tabelle der unregelmäßigen Verben.

1	fall	fell	fallen
2		bit	
3	bring		
4			read
5		chose	
6	wear		

7	fly		
8		bet	
9			led
10		made	
11	pay		
12		won	

New words ► p. 31

I can't ______________ a new car at the moment.	Ich kann **mir** im Moment kein neues Auto **leisten**.
There are 60 ______________ in a minute.	Eine Minute hat 60 **Sekunden**.
Coal and oil are ______________.	Kohle und Öl sind **fossile Brennstoffe**.
______________ energy comes from the sun.	**Solar**energie kommt von der Sonne.
Coal power stations cause air ______________.	Kohlekraftwerke verursachen Luft**verschmutzung**.
There's no 'ä' on my computer ______________.	Auf meiner Computer**tastatur** gibt es kein „ä“.
Too much alcohol kills your ______________ cells.	Zu viel Alkohol tötet die **Gehirn**zellen.
The ______________ showed interesting results.	Das **Experiment** zeigte interessante Ergebnisse.

6 The best word

Finde das Wort A, B, C oder D, das am besten in die Lücke passt.

A heat	**B** pollute	**C** cause	**D** release	1 Cars still ______________ too much carbon dioxide.
A attract	**B** afford	**C** allow	**D** advise	2 We can't ______________ such an expensive house.
A brains	**B** batteries	**C** budgies	**D** gadgets	3 How do we actually create thoughts in our ______________?
A apprentice	**B** application	**C** appliance	**D** appearance	4 A washing machine is a useful electric ______________.
A invention	**B** invitation	**C** insulation	**D** institution	5 Isn't the mobile phone a great ______________?
A revolutions	**B** conditions	**C** situations	**D** emissions	6 I don't like camping in these weather ______________.

7 Odd word out

Ein Wort passt nicht.
Finde und unterstreiche es.

1 lip – law – ear – nose

2 March – April – may – June

3 brain – heart – carbon – eye

4 coal – oil – gas – solar

5 first – second – minute – hour

6 target – power – energy – electricity

7 dirt – choice – rubbish – pollution

8 keyboard – mouse – hamster – screen

New words ▸ pp. 32–33

__________ gadgets make housework easier.	**Haushalts**geräte erleichtern die Hausarbeit.
For this disease you have to take __________.	Bei dieser Krankheit musst du **Antibiotika** nehmen.
Columbus' __________ of America was in 1492.	Kolumbus' **Entdeckung** von Amerika war 1492.
Stay away – the disease is highly __________.	Bleib weg – die Krankheit ist hoch **ansteckend**.
She studied __________ to become a doctor.	Sie studierte **Medizin**, um Arzt zu werden.
__________ is an antibiotic.	**Penizillin** ist ein Antibiotikum.
New drugs are often __________ on mice.	Neue Medikamente werden oft an Mäusen **getestet**.
The book's called 'London now and __________'.	Das Buch heißt „London heute und **damals**".
The found fossil __________ of a dinosaur.	Sie fanden fossile **Knochen** eines Dinosauriers.
The __________ shows the broken bone.	Das **Röntgenbild** zeigt den gebrochenen Knochen.
__________ my teacher I've learned a lot.	Ich habe **dank** meines Lehres viel gelernt.
Suddenly she __________ what had happened.	Plötzlich **wurde** ihr **bewusst**, was passiert war.
You can download this little __________.	Man kann diese kleine **Anwendung** herunterladen.

8 Word families

a) Finde die passenden Nomen zu den angegebenen Verben.

1 pollute – __________	*5* test – __________	*9* invent – __________
2 enquire – __________	*6* bet – __________	*10* cause – __________
3 discuss – __________	*7* react – __________	*11* believe – __________
4 discover – __________	*8* heat – __________	*12* choose – __________

b) Vervollständige die Sätze mit der korrekten Form eines Verbs oder Nomens aus a).

1 Should new drugs always be __________ on animals?

2 The technicians couldn't find the __________ of the problem.

3 Was America really first __________ by Columbus?

4 ManU won – that means I've lost my __________ with Steve!

5 Hello! I'd like to __________ about the prices of your hotel rooms.

6 We must stop the __________ of our environment!

New words ▸ p. 34

We all should __________ our carbon footprint.	Wir sollten alle unsere CO_2-Bilanz **verringern.**
Can you ________ me __________ this form?	Kannst du dieses Formular **mit mir durchgehen**?
I can't carry the suitcase – it's too __________.	Ich kann den Koffer nicht tragen – er ist zu **schwer.**
Her __________ at home has a great sound.	Ihre **Stereoanlage** zuhause hat einen tollen Klang.
This soap opera seems to go __________!	Diese Seifenoper scheint **immer weiter** zu gehen!
Talking about sex is a __________ in her family.	Über Sex zu sprechen ist **tabu** in ihrer Familie.
He solved the problems __________.	Er löste **ein** Problem **nach dem anderen.**
She looked for the key, but it was __________.	Sie suchte den Schlüssel, aber er war **weg.**
She __________ not to know her ex-boyfriend.	Sie **tat so, als ob** sie ihren Ex-Freund nicht kenne.
__________ the card here to open the door.	**Zieh** die Karte hier **durch**, um die Tür zu öffnen.
He was wearing a long winter __________.	Er trug einen langen Winter**mantel.**
Who's __________ for the mistake?	Wer ist für den Fehler **verantwortlich**?

9 Lost words

Ergänze die Sätze mit der jeweils korrekten Präposition.
Bei einem der Sätze bleibt die Lücke leer.

1 Jane is __________ the chemist's to get some medicine.
2 I don't think we can afford __________ a new car.
3 You can only communicate __________ Marc by e-mail.
4 £1,000 is a large amount __________ money.
5 Who's responsible __________ this dangerous experiment?
6 He can play nice tunes __________ his keyboard.
7 Thanks __________ penicillin we can fight infectious diseases.
8 You can only download the files one __________ one.
9 So tell me more __________ this application.
10 Can you please take me __________ this form?
11 There are seven days __________ a week.
12 After ten years she was released __________ prison.

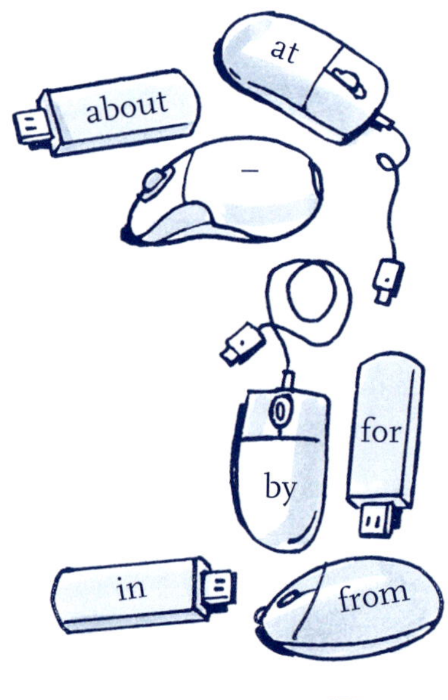

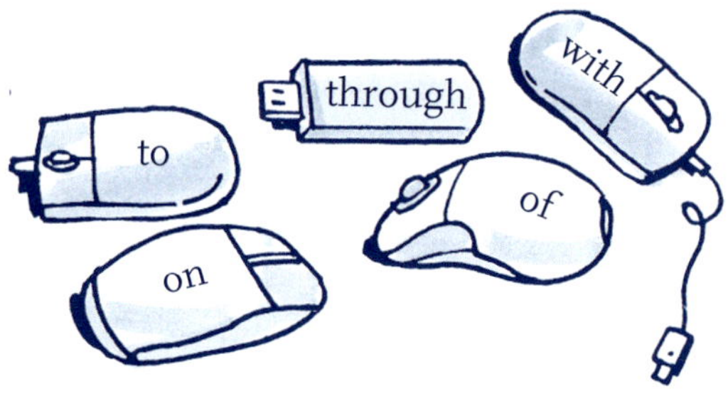

New words ▸ p. 35

She ______________ in tears at the funeral.	Sie **brach** beim Begräbnis in Tränen **zusammen.**
Dan misses you – he ________ asking about you.	Dan vermisst dich – er fragt **immer wieder** nach dir.
Winters in Alaska are ____________ cold.	Die Winter in Alaska sind **eis**kalt.
The taxi driver tried to ______ the tourist _____ .	Der Taxifahrer versuchte den Tourist **abzuzocken.**
It's the old story of good against ________ .	Es ist die alte Geschichte von Gut gegen **Böse.**
He has no free time – he works __________ .	Er hat keine Freizeit – er arbeitet **rund um die Uhr.**
A man came to read the gas __________ .	Ein Mann kam, um den Gas**zähler** abzulesen.
Ice will __________ in the sun.	Eis **schmilzt** in der Sonne.
The lights went off because of a ____________ .	Die Lichter gingen aus wegen eines **Stromausfalls.**
This dark old castle gives me the __________ .	Dieses dunkle, alte Schloss ist mir **unheimlich.**

10 Word building

Verbinde die Wörter 1–10 mit jeweils einem passenden Wort aus der Mauer. Achte dabei auf die Schreibweise (getrennt oder zusammen), und trage die deutsche Übersetzung ein.

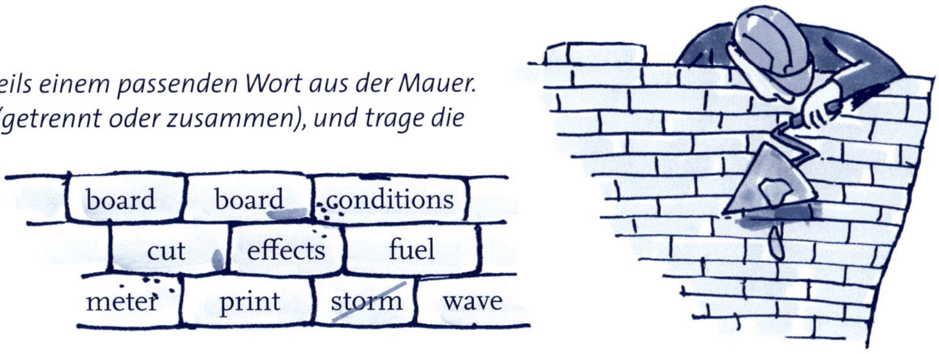

1 snowstorm ________ ________________

2 living________ ________________

3 special________ ________________

4 micro________ ________________

5 fossil________ ________________

6 gas________ ________________

7 foot________ ________________

8 white________ ________________

9 power________ ________________

10 key________ ________________

11 The fourth word

Welches Wort fehlt hier?

1 see – eyes think – ______________

2 turn – key swipe – ______________

3 time – clock gas – ______________

4 bread – food penicillin – ______________

5 kilometre – metre tonne – ______________

6 toaster – appliances coat – ______________

7 hero – good monster – ______________

8 today – years ago now – ______________

New words ▸ p. 36 (part 1)

Even small things can make ________________ .	Selbst kleine Dinge können etwas **bewirken.**
Temperatures are very __________ in Alaska.	Die Temperaturen sind sehr **niedrig** in Alaska.
You need three ________________ for this lamp.	Man braucht drei **Glühbirnen** für diese Lampe.
The battery was in the __________ – now it's full.	Die Batterie war im **Ladegerät** – jetzt ist sie voll.
You can't ______________ under water.	Unter Wasser kann man nicht **atmen.**
A farmer works in ________________ .	Ein Bauer arbeitet in der **Landwirtschaft.**

12 Word pairs

Welche Wörter passen zusammen?

1) carbon
2) climate
3) (to) download
4) freezing
5) light
6) (to) make
7) (to) reach
8) solar
9) (to) swipe
10) (to) work

24/7
an app
a card
a difference
bulb
change
cold
emissions
power
a target

13 Making new words

Bilde aus den Buchstaben des Wortes so viele neue Wörter wie möglich. Wenn du zehn Wörter findest: nicht schlecht. 20 Wörter: sehr gut. 30 oder mehr Wörter: absolute Spitze!

age, girl,

agriculture

New words ▸ *pp. 36 (part 2) – 37*

Modern food is sometimes full of ____________ .	Modernes Essen ist manchmal voller **Chemikalien**.
__________ vegetables are expensive but healthy.	**Bio**-Gemüse ist teuer, aber gesund.
Less ________________ means less rubbish.	Weniger **Verpackung** bedeutet weniger Müll.
Have you paid the gas ________ this month?	Hast du die Gas**rechnung** diesen Monat bezahlt?
Oh no! I had ____________ forgotten about it!	Oh nein! Das hatte ich **völlig** vergessen!
To build the road, 50 trees were ____________ .	Um die Straße zu bauen, wurden 50 Bäume **gefällt**.
On the one ______ I agree, on the ______ I don't.	**Einerseits** stimme ich zu, **andererseits** nicht.

14 Words with different meanings

Finde die passende englische Übersetzung zu den unterstrichenen deutschen Wörtern auf den Zetteln 1 – 9.

1)
a) Einerseits ist das Auto schneller, anderer<u>seits</u> aber auch teurer.
b) Ich habe mir die <u>Hand</u> gebrochen.
____

2)
a) Nicht alle Vampire in dem Film sind <u>böse</u>.
b) Dieser Geruch ist wirklich <u>übel</u>!
____

3)
a) Die Tasche ist zu <u>schwer</u> für mich.
b) Sie ist eine <u>starke</u> Raucherin.
____

4)
a) Ich <u>bin mir bewusst</u>, dass es schwierig werden kann.
b) Können wir das Projekt <u>verwirklichen</u>?
____

5)
a) <u>Gas</u> und Strom werden immer teurer.
b) Bei uns in den USA gibt es billigeres <u>Benzin</u>.
____

6)
a) Du brauchst nur eine kleine <u>Menge</u> Salz.
b) Ich musste nicht den vollen <u>Betrag</u> zahlen.
____

7)
a) Warte – es dauert nur eine <u>Sekunde</u>!
b) Das ist jetzt der <u>zweite</u> Versuch.
____

8)
a) Sie ist gerade nach Hause <u>gegangen</u>.
b) Oh nein – meine Tasche ist <u>weg</u>!
____

9)
a) Können wir bitte die <u>Rechnung</u> haben?
b) Ich habe noch einen 10-Dollar-<u>Schein</u>.
____

15 More about … Global Warming

Vervollständige den Text mit den passenden Wörtern aus der Box.

carbon – climate – coal – deserts – effects – energy – footprint – fossil – heating – homes – ice – islands – storms – temperature

The earth's global (1) ______________ is rising fast. More and more people on this planet are using more and more (2) ______________, which is mostly produced by burning (3) ______________ fuels like oil, gas or (4) ______________. This releases a lot of (5) ______________ dioxide into the atmosphere and finally leads to (6) ______________ change.

But why is global warming so bad? There are many negative (7) ______________. Sea levels are rising because the earth's (8) ______________ is melting. Lots of small (9) ______________, but also low-lying countries like the Netherlands, are in danger. Most (10) ______________ will get bigger because there will be less rain. In other places there will be more rain and heavier (11) ______________. Millions of people will lose their (12) ______________, and lots of animals will disappear forever.

Can we stop it? At least we can all try to reduce our carbon (13) ______________. All the modern technology we use causes CO_2 emissions – so think twice about whether you really need to turn up the (14) ______________ or play video games all day!

16 What are the words?

Wie übersetzt man die fettgedruckten Wörter ins Deutsche?

1 Put on this coat – it will **keep** you warm ______________

2 She **keeps** all her old photos in this box. ______________

3 I'm trying to phone her, but the line **keeps** breaking down. ______________

4 It was good to see you again – let's **keep in touch**. ______________

5 I don't need the magazine anymore – you can **keep** it. ______________

17 Two-part verbs

Vervollständige die Sätze mit einem passenden Wort von den USB-Sticks.

1 When does the bus leave? – Wait, I'll look it ______________ on the Internet.

2 Bill and Kate have been going ______________ for some time now.

3 He feels really bad – he broke ______________ with Sue yesterday.

4 Breathe in normally, and then breathe ______________ slowly.

5 I can't come to see you – my car has broken ______________ .

6 Don't go to that restaurant – they just rip you ______________ !

7 Isn't steel made ______________ of different metals?

8 She fell ______________ on the ice and broke her hand.

9 I think we have to get ______________ at the next stop.

10 Global warming will become worse if we cut ______________ all the forests.

18 Word search: Health and illness

Finde 16 Begriffe aus dem Wortfeld „Gesundheit und Krankheiten". (↓ →) Übersetze sie ins Deutsche.

P	D	Y	G	D	O	C	T	O	R
S	R	H	O	S	P	I	T	A	L
H	U	D	I	S	E	A	S	E	M
E	G	D	E	S	R	L	U	P	E
A	M	B	U	L	A	N	C	E	D
D	G	J	H	O	T	C	J	N	I
A	N	T	I	B	I	O	T	I	C
C	V	Q	R	K	O	L	G	C	I
H	N	H	R	S	N	D	F	I	N
E	J	C	A	N	C	E	R	L	E
C	H	E	M	I	S	T	B	L	K
E	P	A	R	A	M	E	D	I	C
R	D	E	N	T	I	S	T	N	V
I	N	F	E	C	T	I	O	U	S

doctor – Arzt/Ärztin

B 6 Unit 3

New words ▸ p. 46

Your opinion is important – have ____________!	Deine Meinung ist wichtig – **rede mit!**
We should discuss this important __________.	Wir sollten dieses wichtige **Thema** diskutieren.
I really __________ about the environment.	Mir **ist** die Umwelt wirklich **wichtig.**
We had no money – we lived in ____________.	Wir hatten kein Geld – wir lebten in **Armut.**
Our school has excellent sports ________________.	Unsere Schule hat ausgezeichnete Sport**anlagen.**

1 Crossword

Trage die Übersetzungen der deutschen Wörter ins Rätsel ein.

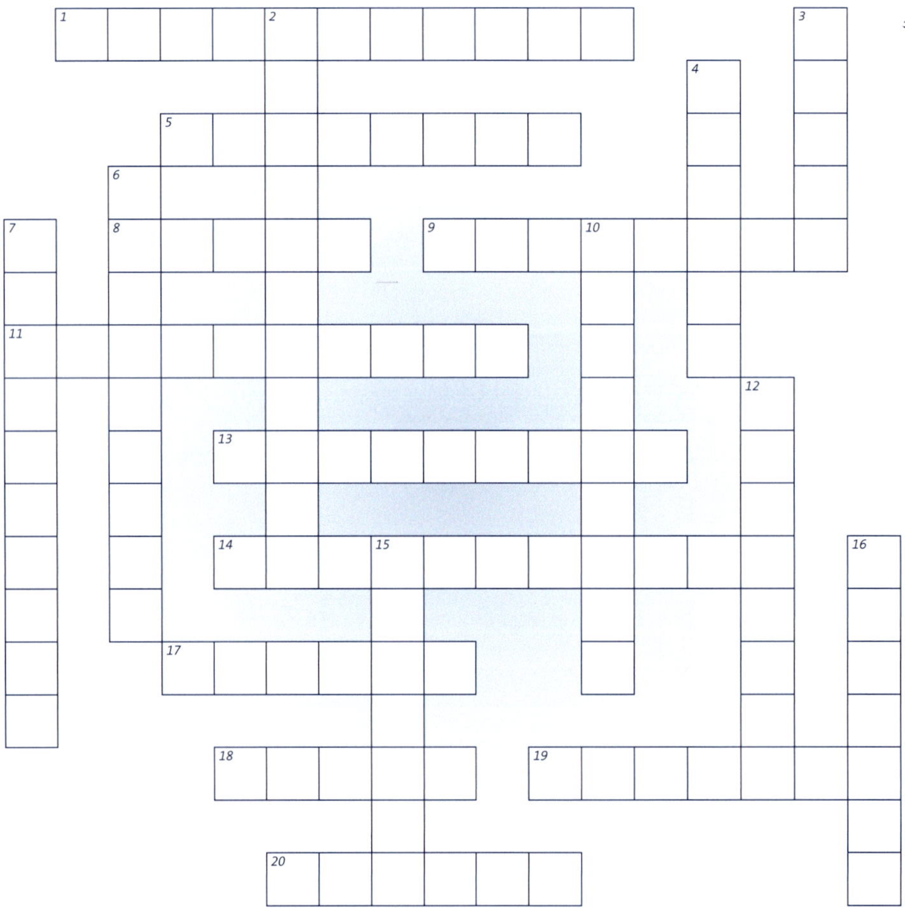

Across
(1) Landwirtschaft
(5) vollständig, komplett
(8) Thema, (Streit-)Frage
(9) Beweglichkeit, Mobilität
(11) Einrichtungen, Anlagen
(13) Verpackung
(14) verantwortlich
(17) Ziel(scheibe)
(18) Zähler
(19) Ladegerät
(20) verringern, reduzieren

Down
(2) sich verständigen, kommunizieren
(3) schwer/heftig
(4) Wahl, Auswahl
(6) Entdeckung
(7) ansteckend
(10) Erfindung
(12) eisig, eiskalt
(15) so tun, als ob
(16) Armut

New words ►p. 47 (part 1)

Global __________ is growing, especially with China.	Der globale **Handel** wächst, vor allem mit China.
Leave a mobile __________ till the battery is full.	Lass ein Handy **am Netz**, bis die Batterie voll ist.
It takes an hour to __________ the batteries.	Es dauert eine Stunde, um die Batterien zu **laden**.
Finally her greatest __________ came true.	Schließlich wurde ihr größter **Wunsch** wahr.
I really __________ for a better world.	Ich **wünsche** mir wirklich eine bessere Welt.
One student __________ about the difficult test.	Ein Student **beklagte sich** über den schweren Test.
I'm not telling lies – it's the sad __________.	Ich lüge nicht – es ist die traurige **Wahrheit**.
A local __________ became party leader.	Ein Lokal**politiker** wurde Parteiführer.

2 Lost words

Ergänze die Sätze mit der jeweils korrekten Präposition.
Bei einem der Sätze bleibt die Lücke leer.

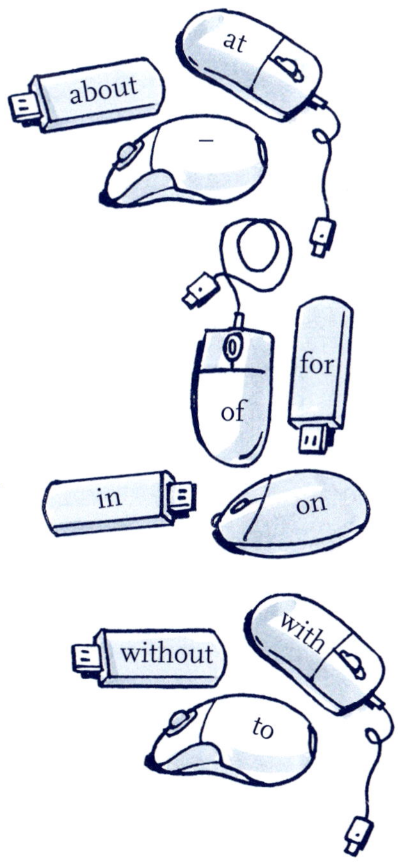

1 Too many people in this world live __________ poverty.

2 I often wish __________ a world where everyone's happy.

3 The air is made up __________ different gases.

4 Organic vegetables are grown __________ chemicals.

5 Shouldn't we all care __________ the environment?

6 She complained __________ the waiter about the bad coffee.

7 Our country does a lot of trade __________ the USA.

8 I can't call her – my mobile's still __________ charge.

9 How long does it take to charge __________ the batteries?

10 Last night __________ nine there was a power cut.

3 Opposites

Trage das Gegenteil der fettgedruckten Wörter in die Lücken ein.

1 **agree** / __________ with someone

2 tell someone **lies** / the __________

3 have **high** / __________ temperatures

4 be **tolerant** / __________ of others

5 I can't sleep in this **cold** / __________

6 a **poor** / __________ country

7 on the **one** / __________ hand

8 a **thick** / __________ soup

New words ► *p. 47 (part 2)*

If you see a problem, ________________ !	Wenn du ein Problem siehst, **sag deine Meinung**!
They started a __________ against the motorway.	Sie erstellten eine **Petition** gegen die Autobahn.
We've started a _____________ for animal rights.	Wir haben eine **Kampagne** für Tierrechte gestartet.
Please __________ the form here.	Bitte **unterschreiben** Sie das Formular hier..
It's very __________ that the oil price will go up.	Es ist sehr **wahrscheinlich**, dass der Ölpreis steigt.
At that time of year it's __________ to snow.	Zu der Jahreszeit schneit es **wahrscheinlich**.
He tells everyone what to do – he's so _________ !	Er sagt jedem, was er tun soll – er ist so **herrisch**!
It was very _____________ of you to pick me up.	Es war sehr **aufmerksam** von dir, mich abzuholen.

4 The best word

Finde das Wort A, B, C oder D, das am besten in die Lücke passt.

A write, B skim, C sign, D wish	*1* You have to _____________ the petition at the bottom.
A inventions, B issues, C brains, D gadgets	*2* Saving the planet is one of the big _____________ today.
A facilities, B fantasies, C batteries, D discoveries	*3* There are some good free-time _____________ in our town.
A completed, B competed, C complained, D compared	*4* He _____________ about the food because it was cold.
A bossy, B helpful, C heavy, D thoughtful	*5* What's wrong with Dan? He's looking so _____________ .
A charity, B charger, C chart, D channel	*6* You need a special _____________ for these batteries.

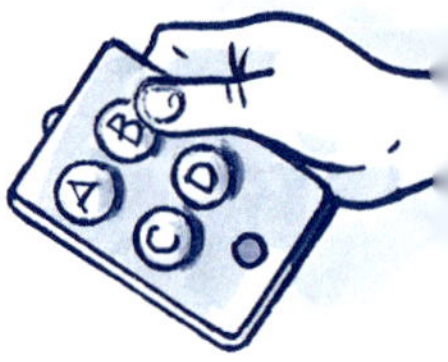

5 Making new words

Bilde aus den Buchstaben des Wortes so viele neue Wörter wie möglich.
20 Wörter solltest du leicht finden, aber wer findet über 40?

facilities

act, castle,

New words ▸ p. 48

I can't ________ this silly idea ____________!	Ich kann diese dumme Idee nicht **ernst nehmen**!
The shy star never appears in ________.	Der scheue Star erscheint nie in der **Öffentlichkeit**.
What have I done to __________ this?	Was habe ich getan, dass ich das **verdiene**?
We want ________ rights for men and women.	Wir wollen **gleiche** Rechte für Männer und Frauen.
I can't do two things ____________!	Ich kann nicht zwei Sachen **auf einmal** machen!
We will have the barbecue – ________ it rains.	Wir machen das Grillfest – **es sei denn**, es regnet.

6 Word families

a) Finde die passenden Nomen zu den angegebenen Adjektiven.

1 different – ____________ *5* true – ____________ *9* mobile – ____________

2 religious – ____________ *6* poor – ____________ *10* public – ____________

3 political – ____________ *7* racist – ____________ *11* strong – ____________

4 confident – ____________ *8* real – ____________ *12* happy – ____________

b) Vervollständige die Sätze mit der korrekten Form eines Adjektivs oder Nomens aus a).

1 Everything he said was right – he told the ______________!

2 She reads the Bible, goes to church and is very ______________.

3 Does it make a ______________ whether I vote or not?

4 Please tell us one of your ______________ and one of your weaknesses.

5 I've been much more ______________ since I've had a car!

7 Two-part verbs

Vervollständige die Sätze mit einem passenden Wort von den USB-Sticks.

1 Please turn ____________ the stereo, Mike – we need to go now.

2 It took a day to straighten ____________ the house after the party.

3 It was quite warm, so he took ____________ his pullover.

4 If you want to change something, you have to speak ____________!

5 I never know how to chat someone ____________.

6 Who do you normally hang ____________ with?

New words ▸ *p. 49 (part 1)*

________ when you do it – just do it!	**Es spielt keine Rolle**, wann du es tust – nur tue es!
These dirty toilets smell ________!	Diese schmutzigen Toiletten riechen **ekelhaft**!
Every night I was bitten by ________.	Jede Nacht wurde ich von **Moskitos** gestochen.
GPS is a useful ________ for the car.	GPS ist eine nützliche **Vorrichtung** fürs Auto.
I find it ________ when people are late.	Ich finde es **lästig**, wenn Leute zu spät kommen.
The noise is really beginning to ________ me.	Der Krach beginnt mich wirklich zu **stören**.
This sentence doesn't ________ in English.	Dieser Satz **ergibt** auf Englisch **keinen Sinn**.

8 Odd word out

Ein Wort passt nicht.
Finde und unterstreiche es.

1 pen – (to) sign – charger – paper

2 disgusting – evil – bad – romantic

3 appliance – campaign – device – gadget

4 application – program – medicine – software

5 coat – bone – suit – jacket

6 wish – issue – topic – question

7 same – similar – equal – lazy

8 bossy – insect – bite – mosquito

9 Pronunciation

Ordne die Wörter der richtigen Aussprachegruppe zu, je nachdem, wie der unterstrichene Vokal ausgesprochen wird.

~~bill~~ reduce evil disgusting breathe deserve heat device creeps meter pretend hit wish issue speak rip off freezing complete equal lead

ɪ	iː
bill	

New words ▸ p. 49 (part 2)

These changes do not directly __________ you.	Diese Änderungen **betreffen** dich nicht direkt.
After school he joined the US __________ .	Nach der Schule ging er zur US **Armee**.
The government wants higher __________ on fuel.	Die Regierung will höhere **Steuern** auf Kraftstoff.
I'm too old. – Oh, __________ that's not true!	Ich bin zu alt. – Ach, das ist **doch sicher** nicht wahr!
His English will __________ in England.	Sein Englisch wird sich in England **verbessern**.
She __________ him for not working enough.	Sie **kritisierte** ihn, dass er nicht genug arbeite.
The rule isn't silly – it's very __________ .	Die Regel ist nicht dumm – sie ist sehr **vernünftig**.

10 Definitions

Vervollständige die Definitionen mit Wörtern von dem Laptop-Monitor.
Trage die richtige Lösung von den USB-Sticks in die rechte Spalte ein.

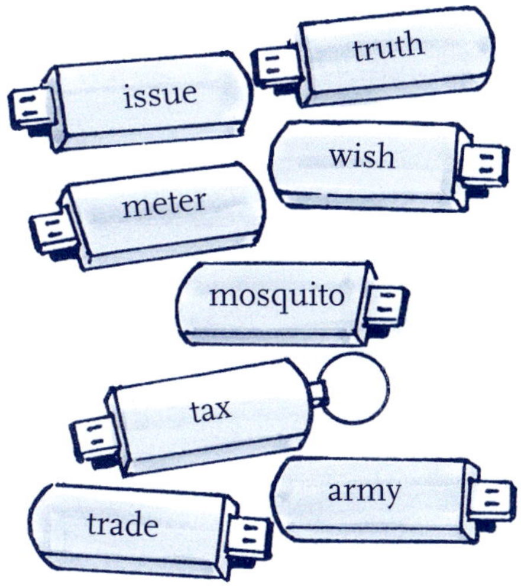

1 a flying __________ that bites humans and __________ __________

2 __________ that you have to pay to the __________ __________

3 a __________ of soldiers who are trained to fight on __________ __________

4 a __________ that shows how much gas or __________ you have used __________

5 the __________ of buying and selling by people or __________ __________

6 the __________ that you want __________ to happen __________

7 an important __________ that people argue about in a __________ __________

8 the real __________ about a situation, event or __________ __________

New words ▸ pp. 50–51

First-class train __________ are higher.	Zug**fahrpreise** erster Klasse sind höher.
Let's ______________ now and save the planet!	Lasst uns jetzt **handeln** und den Planeten retten!
They __________ a meeting every Monday at ten.	Jeden Montag um zehn **halten** sie eine Sitzung **ab**.
The office was at the end of a long __________.	Das Büro war am Ende eines langen **Gangs**.
Who is the ______________ of the discussion?	Wer ist der **Moderator** für die Diskussion?
She didn't feel ______________ in her tight dress.	Sie fühlte sich nicht **wohl** in ihrem engen Kleid.

11 Verb forms

Ergänze die Tabelle der unregelmäßigen Verben.

1	make	made	made
2			done
3		got	
4	speak		
5		held	

6	keep		
7		had	
8			taken
9		gave	
10	break		

12 Word pairs

Welche Wörter passen am besten zusammen?

1) bus

2) (to) charge

3) (to) deserve

4) equal

5) (to) hold

6) member

7) (to) reduce

8) school

9) sensible

10) (to) tell

a battery
corridor
fare
a holiday
a meeting
of parliament
plan
pollution
rights
the truth

New words ▸ p. 54

'-ness' and '-ity' are two English ____________.	„-ness“ und „-ity“ sind zwei englische **Nachsilben**.
Many foreigners ______________ to this country.	Viele Ausländer **wandern** in dieses Land **ein**.
Is there much illegal ______________ to the US?	Gibt es viel illegale **Einwanderung** in die USA?
Be quiet – I want to ______________ on the film.	Sei still – ich will mich auf den Film **konzentrieren**.
Losing your ______________ leads to mistakes.	Die **Konzentration** zu verlieren führt zu Fehlern.
Say it! You have the right to ______________.	Sag es! Du hast das Recht auf **Redefreiheit**.

13 Words with a similar meaning

Finde Wörter, die das Gleiche bedeuten wie die fettgedruckten Wörter. Trage sie ein und schreibe die deutsche Übersetzung auf.

1 Let's make a difference and **do something** / take action ! etwas unternehmen

2 Every week we **have** / ______________ at least one meeting. ______________

3 If you go to the UK, your English will **become better** / ______________. ______________

4 This is a useful **gadget** / ______________ for killing mosquitos. ______________

5 I'd like to enquire about train **ticket prices** / ______________. ______________

6 Sometimes men and women don't get **the same** / ______________ pay. ______________

7 I don't know where Tom is – **perhaps** / ______________ in the corridor? ______________

8 You can download the **full** / ______________ program from the Internet. ______________

14 Spot the mistakes

In jedem Satz sind zwei Fehler. Unterstreiche und korrigiere sie.

1 He only eats biology food, but on the other side he smokes. ______________ ______________

2 Please leaf me alone – I need to concentrate me on my work. ______________ ______________

3 He's a popular TV moderator, but he gives me the crepes. ______________ ______________

4 Jane always crys so much – I think she's just too sensible. ______________ ______________

5 It don't matter whether you believe it or not – it's the trueth. ______________ ______________

6 What this politician says in the public is quite anoying. ______________ ______________

7 We should take climate change serious – it effects all of us. ______________ ______________

New words ▸ p. 55

The war is a __________ between two cultures.	Der Krieg ist ein **Konflikt** zwischen zwei Kulturen.
She finally didn't __________ the job.	Schließlich **nahm** sie den Job nicht **an**.
He accepted her __________ for her behaviour.	Er nahm ihre **Entschuldigung** für ihr Verhalten an.
Is it really OK? – Sure, __________!	Ist das wirklich OK? – Sicher, **kein Problem**!
I'm so sorry – I didn't __________ to hurt you!	Es tut mir so leid – ich **wollte** dir nicht wehtun!
I'm tired – I __________ slept longer.	Ich bin müde – ich **hätte** länger schlafen **sollen**.
Can I __________ with you? It's important.	Kann ich mal **kurz** mit dir **reden**? Es ist wichtig.

15 The fourth word

Welches Wort fehlt hier?

1	bottle – fill	battery – __________	*6*	players – team	soldiers – __________
2	live – life	immigrate – __________	*7*	explain – explanation	apologize – __________
3	fire – candle	electricity – __________	*8*	discuss – discussion	concentrate – __________
4	small – big	low – __________	*9*	dangerous – danger	chemical – __________
5	closed – private	open – __________	*10*	science – scientist	politics – __________

16 Word friends

Auf jedem Plakat gibt es drei Wörter/Wortverbindungen, die direkt nach dem Verb auf dem kleinen Zettel folgen können. Unterstreiche sie.

17 Word search: Science and technology

Finde 18 Begriffe aus dem Wortfeld „Wissenschaft und Technologie“. Übersetze sie ins Deutsche. (↓ →)

I	E	M	I	S	S	I	O	N	S	P	F	I	P	L	I	B	D
A	P	P	L	I	C	A	T	I	O	N	U	N	N	T	O	A	I
A	A	P	P	L	I	A	N	C	E	D	E	V	I	C	E	T	S
T	I	M	I	L	E	S	T	O	N	E	L	E	C	A	S	T	C
H	E	A	T	I	N	G	G	T	I	C	O	N	S	O	L	E	O
C	O	M	P	U	T	E	R	A	C	O	C	T	D	A	P	R	V
S	O	L	A	R	I	E	L	E	C	T	R	I	C	I	T	Y	E
P	O	W	E	R	S	R	M	M	I	C	R	O	W	A	V	E	R
G	A	D	G	E	T	M	W	L	V	T	R	N	L	N	I	E	Y

device – Vorrichtung

18 Word stress

Unterstreiche bei allen Wörtern die Silbe, die betont werden muss.

accept	affect	apology	army
chemical	comfortable	company	complain
conflict	criticize	emission	experiment
facilities	issue	medicine	moderator
penicillin	politician	revolution	solar

Revision: Word groups

Ordne den vier Oberbegriffen auf den Laptops jeweils sechs passende Wörter zu.
Weitere sechs Wörter aus der Box passen zu keinem der Oberbegriffe.

advert – ambulance – ancestor – antibiotic – application – audience – cancer – candidate – certificate – colony – disease – gadget – infectious – interview – museums – outline – packaging – paramedic – projector – reference – screen – sensible – skyscraper – slide – station – tide – theatre – traffic jam – transparency – underground